Diabetes Mellitus in Unani Medicine: An Integrative Approach

"UNANI INSIGHT IN TO DIABETES"

Dr. BUSHRA SHAIKH

Prof. GHULAMUDDIN SOFI

Dr. SHARIQ-UR-RAHIM SHAIKH

DEDICATION

To the wisdom of the past and the innovation of the present, inspiring health and healing for all.

Acknowledgement

First and foremost, I extend my deepest gratitude to **Almighty Allah (SWT)** for endless blessings, guidance, and mercy throughout my journey. Without grace, this work would not have been possible.

I am profoundly grateful to my beloved parents *Janab Abdul Rahman Shaikh Sahab* and *Mohtarma Nasreen Saheba*, whose unwavering love and encouragement have been the foundation of my pursuits. Their sacrifices and belief in my potential have inspired me to strive for excellence in all that I do.

To my Guide and teacher **Prof. Ghulammudin Sofi Sir**, thank you for imparting your wisdom and nurturing my curiosity. Your guidance has shaped my understanding of Unani medicine and has been instrumental in the development of this book.

I also want to thank my teachers and mentors **Prof. Sayyad Shah Alam Sir** Director NIUM Bangalore, **Prof. Aleemuddin Qumri sir**, **Prof. Abdul Wadood sir, Prof. Nasreen Jahan Maam**, **Prof. Najeeb Jahan Maam**, **Dr. Imran sir, Dr. Hamiduddin sir, Dr.Shariq Shamsi sir (**NIUM Bengalore), **Prof. Akhtar Hussain Farooqui sir** (Principal ZVM Pune), **Prof. Iftekhar sir** (HZS Unani medical college Bhopal), **Prof. Saquib Hussain sir** (AGU medical college Akkalkuwa) **Dr. Rukhsana Maam** (Principal TSUMCH Gulbarga),Your guidance, advice and helpful feedback have been so important in shaping my idea , I have learn a lot from all of you ,and you have inspired me to think deeply.

I would also like to express my heartfelt appreciation to my uncle *Janab Maheboob Khan Sahab*, whose encouragement and support have been invaluable. His insights and blessings have motivated me to achieve my goal.

To my **brothers**, *Dr.Sharique-Ur-Rahim Shaikh* and *Dr.Mohsin Iqbal Shaikh* thank you for your constant help during this phase it may be technical, literal, moral encouragement and camaraderie. Your belief in me has provided strength during challenging times.

I also extend my heartfelt thanks to **Dr. Iliyas Hussain** for his time to time help regarding publication of this book.

Lastly, I extend my gratitude to my **Teachers**, **family** and **friends** for their unwavering support and understanding. Your encouragement has been a source of inspiration, reminding me that I am never alone in this journey.

This book is a testament to the collective support of all these remarkable individuals. Thank you for being part of this journey with me.

Foreword

Diabetes mellitus, a condition that has grown into a global health challenge, demands innovative and integrative solutions to its prevention and management. While modern medicine has made significant strides in addressing this complex disease, traditional medical systems like Unani Medicine offer profound insights and complementary approaches that are often overlooked. Rooted in centuries-old wisdom, Unani Medicine provides a holistic framework for understanding and managing diabetes by focusing on restoring balance within the body.

Dr. Bushra Sheikh's book, Diabetes Mellitus in Unani Medicine: An Integrative Approach, is a remarkable contribution to this field. It bridges the gap between ancient healing traditions and contemporary science, offering a comprehensive exploration of how Unani principles can be applied to diabetes care. The book delves into the conceptual underpinnings of Unani Medicine, which views diabetes (referred to as "Ziyābetus") as an imbalance in the body's humors—blood, phlegm, yellow bile, and black bile—and altered organ temperaments. This book provides a detailed analysis of how these imbalances manifest as symptoms and how they can be addressed through personalized dietary modifications, lifestyle changes, herbal remedies, and traditional therapeutic procedures.

What sets this work apart is its integrative approach, Dr. Sheikh critically evaluates the scientific evidence supporting Unani practices in diabetes management, presenting a balanced perspective that highlights both their potential benefits and limitations. By synthesizing traditional knowledge with modern research, this book not only underscores the relevance of Unani Medicine in today's healthcare landscape but also opens new avenues for interdisciplinary collaboration.

This book is an invaluable resource for healthcare professionals, researchers, and anyone interested in holistic approaches to diabetes care. It serves as both an educational guide and an inspiration for further research into the integration of Unani Medicine with conventional medical practices. Her work reminds us that the wisdom of the past can illuminate pathways to innovative solutions for contemporary health challenges.

It is my hope that this book will spark renewed interest in traditional healing systems and inspire a deeper appreciation for their role in addressing modern health crises like diabetes mellitus.

Prof. GHULAMUDDIN SOFI

Professor, Department of Ilmul Advia

National Institute of Unani Medicine

Bangalore.

Preface

Diabetes mellitus, a chronic metabolic disorder, has emerged as one of the most pressing global health concerns of our time. Despite the remarkable advancements in modern medicine, the complexity of this disease necessitates a broader and more integrative approach to its prevention and management. Traditional medical systems, such as Unani Medicine, offer invaluable insights into understanding and addressing diabetes through holistic principles that emphasize balance and harmony within the body.

This book, Diabetes Mellitus in Unani Medicine: An Integrative Approach, is the culmination of years of research and clinical exploration into the potential of Unani Medicine to complement conventional diabetes care. It is rooted in the philosophy that health is achieved through equilibrium in the body's humors—blood, phlegm, yellow bile, and black bile—and that disruptions in this balance manifest as disease. The Unani perspective on diabetes, or "Ziyābetus," provides a unique lens through which we can understand its pathophysiology and therapeutic strategies.

Our work aims to bridge the gap between ancient wisdom and contemporary science. By critically analyzing traditional Unani practices alongside modern evidence-based research, this book seeks to offer a comprehensive guide to managing diabetes through dietary modifications, lifestyle changes, herbal remedies, and therapeutic procedures. It also highlights recent scientific studies that support the efficacy of certain Unani interventions in improving glycemic control and overall health outcomes.

This book is not only a resource for healthcare professionals and researchers but also an invitation for readers to explore an integrative approach to diabetes care. It is our hope that this work will inspire further research into Unani Medicine's potential role in addressing chronic diseases and foster collaboration between traditional and modern medical systems.

We are deeply grateful to all those who have contributed to this endeavor—our mentors, colleagues, families, and friends—whose support has been instrumental in bringing this project to fruition. May this book serve as a beacon for those seeking holistic solutions to diabetes management and inspire renewed interest in the rich heritage of Unani Medicine.

Dr. Bushra Fasiha Abdul Raheman Shaikh

Ph.D. Scholar, Department of Ilmul Advia

National Institute of Unani Medicine (NIUM), Bangalore

Dr. Shariq-ur-Rahim Shaikh

BUMS, MHA

MIJ Tibbia College, Mumbai.

Prologue

Diabetes mellitus, a condition that has shaped medical discourse for centuries, remains a formidable challenge in contemporary healthcare. It is a disease that transcends cultures and eras, carrying with its profound implications for human health and well-being. From the ancient Greek understanding of "diabetes" as a siphoning disorder to the Unani concept of "Ziyābetus" rooted in humoral imbalance, the journey of comprehending this ailment is as rich and varied as the civilizations that have studied it.

In the Unani tradition, diabetes is not merely a disorder of blood sugar levels; it is seen as a manifestation of deeper disruptions within the body's humors—blood, phlegm, yellow bile, and black bile—and the altered temperament of vital organs. This holistic perspective offers a unique lens through which diabetes can be understood and addressed. It emphasizes restoring harmony within the body through dietary modifications, lifestyle adjustments, herbal remedies, and therapeutic interventions.

This book invites readers to embark on a transformative exploration of diabetes mellitus through the lens of Unani Medicine. It seeks to unravel the historical roots of this ancient healing system while bridging its principles with modern scientific evidence. By delving into the conceptual framework of Unani Medicine, readers will gain insights into how this tradition views diabetes not as an isolated condition but as part of a broader imbalance affecting the entire organism.

Through this integrative approach, we aim to challenge conventional perceptions and expand the possibilities for managing diabetes in today's world. Whether you are a healthcare professional, researcher, or someone seeking holistic solutions to diabetes care, this book offers a comprehensive guide to understanding and applying Unani Medicine's wisdom in addressing this global epidemic.

The journey ahead is one of discovery—a journey that blends ancient knowledge with modern innovation to illuminate new pathways for health and healing. Let us step forward together into this realm of integration and hope.

Introduction

Diabetes mellitus, a global health crisis defined by persistent hyperglycemia, demands multifaceted strategies for effective management. Within the rich tapestry of medical traditions, Unani Medicine or Greco-Arabic medicine, presents a unique, time-honored, and holistic perspective on this condition. This book explores the principles, practices, and potential of Unani Medicine in addressing diabetes, offering insights into an integrative approach to diabetes care.

Rooted in the ancient wisdom of Greek, Roman, and Persian medical systems, Unani Medicine views diabetes – or "Ziyābetus" – as a manifestation of imbalances within the body's fundamental humors: blood, phlegm, yellow bile, and black bile and the altered temperament of the organs.

 It claims that these imbalances disturb natural metabolic processes, leading to the hallmark symptoms of diabetes, such as increased thirst and frequent urination.

This book will guide you through:

The historical context and conceptual framework of Unani Medicine's understanding of diabetes.

Key Unani therapeutic strategies, including dietary modifications, lifestyle adjustments, herbal remedies, and traditional procedures.

The scientific justification and gathering data support the application of Unani Medicine in the management of diabetes, namely Type 2 diabetic mellitus (T2DM).

The potential of Unani Medicine as a complementary or alternative therapy within a comprehensive diabetes management plan.

By bridging the gap between ancient wisdom and modern science, this book aims to provide a comprehensive understanding of Unani Medicine's role in addressing the growing challenge of diabetes mellitus. It is intended for healthcare professionals, researchers, and anyone seeking a holistic and integrative approach to diabetes management.

Chapters Index

Chapter I

Introduction to Diabetes Mellitus in Unani Medicine

A major worldwide health concern is diabetes mellitus, a chronic metabolic disease marked by increased blood sugar levels. Unani medicine, sometimes referred to as Greco-Arabic medicine, provides a distinctive and comprehensive method of treating this illness within the field of traditional medicine. Rooted in ancient Greek, Roman, and Persian medical traditions, Unani Medicine regards diabetes, or "Ziyābetus," as an illness originating from an imbalance in the body's humors—blood, phlegm, yellow bile, and black bile and changed temperament of the organs. It is thought that this imbalance interferes with the body's normal metabolic functions, resulting in symptoms including frequent urination and excessive thirst.

Restoring equilibrium via food adjustments, lifestyle adjustments, herbal medicines, and therapeutic procedures is emphasized by Unani medicine. Important herbal remedies, such as cinnamon, fenugreek, and bitter melon, have long been used to treat the symptoms of diabetes. According to recent research, Unani drugs have the potential to considerably lower postprandial and fasting blood glucose levels, making them a viable adjunct or alternative treatment for the management of Type 2 diabetic mellitus (T2DM). In order to shed light on Unani Medicine's potential as an integrated approach to diabetes treatment, this book explores its philosophical framework, historical context, and therapeutic approaches in treating diabetes mellitus.

Glucose is the main source of energy needed by all of the body's cells. A simple sugar called glucose is produced during the digestion of meals high in carbohydrates. It travels through the bloodstream and gives cells easily accessible energy when they need it.

Diabetes mellitus is a metabolic disorder which occurs when the pancreas fails to produce sufficient insulin or when the insulin resistance appears in body's cells. As a result, glucose cannot be absorbed into the cells and remains in the bloodstream.[1]

This condition is marked by hyperglycemia, glycosuria, and a negative nitrogen balance, primarily caused by either inadequate insulin secretion by the pancreatic beta cells or a reduced sensitivity of insulin receptors to insulin. A deficiency of insulin affects the metabolism of carbohydrates, proteins, and fats and can disrupt water and electrolyte balance. [2]

Rather than being a single disease, diabetes mellitus comprises a group of metabolic disorders that share the common feature of hyperglycemia. This elevated blood glucose level results from defects in insulin secretion, insulin function, or, in most cases, a combination of both. Chronic hyperglycemia and associated metabolic imbalances can lead to secondary complications in multiple organs, particularly the kidneys, eyes, nerves, and blood vessels. Diabetes is characterized by increased fasting and postprandial blood glucose levels and is the most prevalent metabolic disorder.[3],[4],[5] It is a complex condition affecting carbohydrate, protein, and fat metabolism, often leading to premature death due to cardiovascular complications such as heart attacks and strokes. Many experts believe that diabetes, commonly associated with high blood sugar, is more accurately described as a vascular disease that significantly impacts blood vessels throughout the body.

Concepts of Ziyābetus

The term "Diabetes"[6] originates from the Greek word "διαβαίνω", Greek transliteration:

"Diabainō" [7], meaning "passing through," "to run through," or "siphon." It is characterized by excessive thirst, frequent urination, the presence of sugar in urine, increased appetite, and progressive weight loss. [8],[9], [10]

Ziyābetus is widely referenced in Unani medical literature, including *Al Qaanon, Al Hawi,* and *Kamilul Sana'ah.* Unani scholars considered Ziyābetus to be a kidney-related disorder. Arab physicians also described this condition using various terms, such as *Moattasha, Atsha, Intesae Anmas, Zalaqul Kulliya, Dolab, Dawwarah, Barkar, Barkarya,* and *Qaramees.* [9], [11],[12],[13],[14]

According to Unani medicine, ziyābetus Shakari is a condition in which the water consumed by the patient is rapidly excreted through the kidneys without undergoing metabolic processing. It is similar to *Zalqul Meda wa Ama,* where food passes through the stomach and intestines without proper digestion. Patients with this condition experience excessive thirst, consume large amounts of water, and immediately excrete it without metabolic alteration.[15]

In this disorder, the kidneys develop a *Haar Mizaj* (hot temperament), which causes them to absorb water from the blood and quickly transfer it to the urinary bladder due to weakened *Quwate Masika* (retentive power). It has also been suggested that the kidneys draw water from the bloodstream, liver, stomach, and intestines, while the urinary bladder fails to retain any fluid. This process results in excessive thirst (polydipsia). [11],[12],

Chapter II

Background of diabetes

Prior to the mid-19th century, diabetes mellitus was historically regarded as a renal disease. In antiquity, it was recognised as a urinary system disease marked by excessive urine output, and by the first century AD, its clinical signs and severe consequences were thoroughly documented. Galen (129–200) classified it as a kidney-specific ailment due to a lack in its retentive functions. Ancient Indian literature, including the works of Avicenna (980–1037) and Morgagni (1635–1683), noted the sweet taste of diabetic urine, attributed to the unaltered passage of absorbed water and nutrients into the urine.

In 1674, Thomas Willis (1621-1675) was the first to distinguish diabetes from other types of polyuria. He demonstrated this by indicating that diabetic urine possesses a sweet taste, or quasi-melle, which he postulated originated from the blood. A century later, maybe before to or concurrent with the occurrence of sugar in the urine, Matthew Dobson (1732–1784) demonstrated that the sweetness of urine was attributable to sugar, which was also found in the blood. Despite the recognition that diabetes is induced by raised blood sugar levels, the presence of sugar in the urine was still attributed to the kidneys' inability to retain it. In 1889, subcutaneous pancreas transplantation was employed to address experimentally induced diabetes in pancreatectomized canines. Insulin was successfully isolated in 1922.[16] While its importance as a contributor to kidney disease had not been confirmed, this marked the conclusion of the concept that diabetes was a renal disorder. The evidence of the rising incidence of diabetes as a contributor to chronic kidney disease continues to grow, with the association between the two disorders initially recognised in 1936 and subsequently well-documented.Thomas Willis (1621-1675) was the first to differentiate diabetes from other forms of polyuria in 1674. He established this by finding out that diabetic urine has a sweet taste, or quasi-melle, which he believed originates from the blood[17].

Chapter III

Epidemiology of diabetes

A. Prevalence of diabetes in India

The global diabetes epidemic, predominantly driven by type 2 diabetes, is increasingly affecting developing countries. By 2045,[18] it is projected that 152 million people with diabetes will reside in these regions, with a significant portion in the Indian subcontinent and China. India, being the second most populous country, faces a substantial challenge with diabetes, which is exacerbated by rapid urbanization and lifestyle changes.

Current Status:

Prevalence and Projections: As of 2019, India had approximately 77 million people with diabetes, expected to rise to over 134 million by 2045[19] [20]. Recent studies suggest that this number could already be higher, with estimates indicating over 101 million people living with diabetes, accounting for about 11.4% of the population[21].

Undiagnosed Cases: Approximately 57% of individuals with diabetes in India remain undiagnosed[20].

Pre-diabetes:

An estimated 136 million people are at risk of developing diabetes due to pre-diabetes.

Drivers of the Epidemic

Lifestyle Changes: The shift towards sedentary lifestyles and unhealthy diets, coupled with increased obesity, are major contributors to the rising prevalence of diabetes[22].

Urbanization: Urban areas exhibit higher rates of diabetes compared to rural areas, although rural areas are also experiencing an increase due to lifestyle transitions[23].

Ethnic and Genetic Factors: Indians have a higher genetic predisposition to type 2 diabetes, which is exacerbated by environmental changes[20].

B. Challenges and Future Directions

Healthcare Access:

Challenges include limited access to healthcare, lack of awareness about diabetes, and the high cost of treatment .

Prevention Strategies:

Effective health promotion and primary prevention are crucial to manage the diabetes epidemic. This includes improving access to healthcare, enhancing awareness, and promoting lifestyle changes[24].

Future Projections:

By 2045, the number of people with diabetes in India is expected to exceed 134 million, emphasizing the need for urgent action to prevent and manage diabetes[19].

India's diabetes burden is escalating due to lifestyle changes, urbanization, and genetic predispositions.

Addressing these factors through comprehensive healthcare strategies and public awareness campaigns is essential to mitigate the impact of this epidemic.

Risk factors of diabetes mellitus: [25]

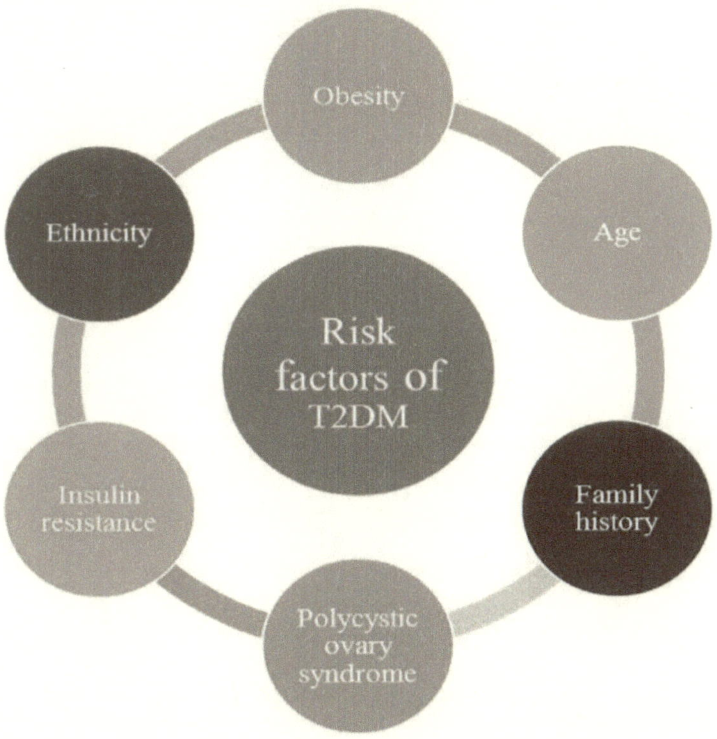

Chapter IV

Diagnostic Criteria for Diabetes:

Diabetes can be identified by many methods. To diagnose diabetes, each procedure generally must be conducted on a subsequent day[26].

Testing must occur in a medical facility, such as a laboratory or a physician's clinic. A physician may not require a second test to diagnose diabetes if a high blood glucose level is detected or if there is one positive test accompanied by common symptoms of elevated blood glucose.

➢ **A1C**

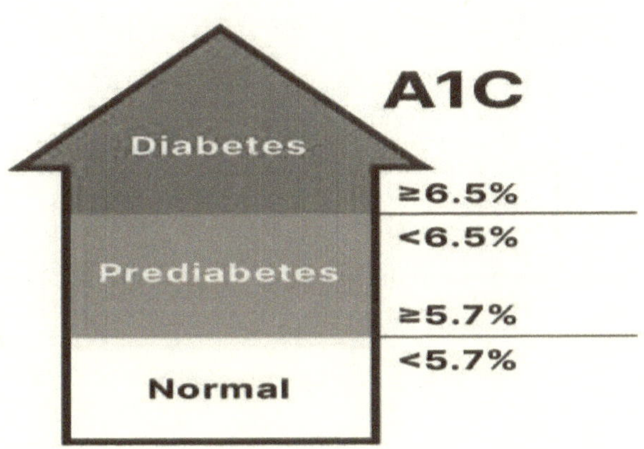

Image Adopted from ADA

Average blood glucose over the last two to three months is measured by the A1C test, which has the benefit of not requiring you to fast or consume any liquids.

Result	A1C
Normal	less than 5.7%
Prediabetic	5.7% to 6.4%
Diabetes	6.5% or higher

Diabetes is diagnosed at an A1C of greater than or equal to 6.5%

> **Fasting Plasma Glucose (FPG)**

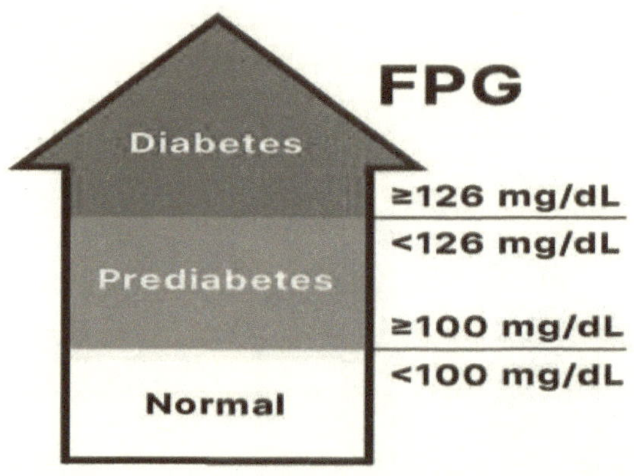

Image Adopted from ADA

Fasting blood glucose levels are measured by this test. Fasting is defined as staying at least eight hours without eating or drinking anything other than water before to the

16

test. Typically, this test is done in the morning, prior to breakfast.

If fasting blood glucose levels are greater than or equal to 126 mg/dl, diabetes is diagnosed.

➤ **Oral Glucose Tolerance Test**

Result	Fasting Plasma Glucose (FPG)
Normal	less than 100 mg/dL
Prediabetes	100 mg/dl to 125 mg/dL
Diabetes	126 mg/dL or higher

(OGTT)

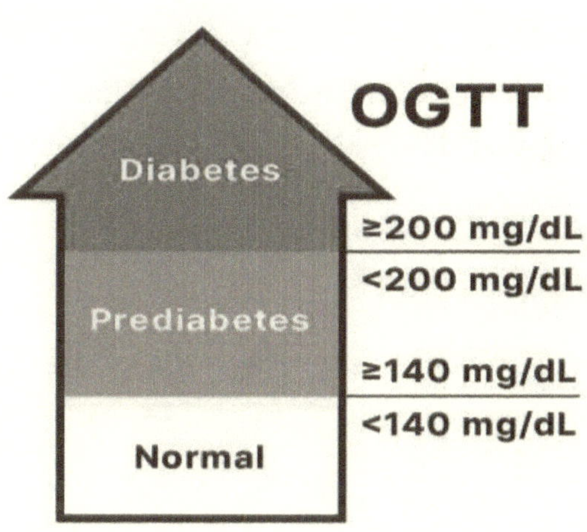

Image Adopted from ADA

The OGTT is a two-hour test that measures your blood sugar levels both before and after consuming a particular sugary drink. It notifies the physician about the way your body handles sugar. Diabetes is diagnosed at two-hour blood glucose of greater than or equal to 200 mg/dl

Result	Oral Glucose Tolerance Test (OGTT)
Normal	less than 140 mg/dL
Prediabetes	140 to 199 mg/dL
Diabetes	200 mg/dL or higher

> **Random (also called Casual) Plasma Glucose Test**

You can undergo this blood test when you have severe symptoms of diabetes, regardless of the time.

Blood glucose levels more than or equal to 200 mg/dl are indicative of diabetes.

What is Prediabetes?

Prediabetes, or blood glucose levels that are higher than usual but not yet high enough to be considered diabetes, is nearly always present before people acquire type 2 diabetes.

Depending on the test performed to identify prediabetes, doctors may refer to it as impaired glucose tolerance (IGT) or impaired fasting glucose (IFG). Developing this condition increases your risk of cardiovascular disease and type 2 diabetes

Symptoms

Prediabetes has no obvious symptoms, so one can be unaware that he or she is having diabetes.

Some prediabetic individuals may already be experiencing some of the signs of diabetes or possibly its complications. When someone undergoes testing for diabetes, we typically discover that they have prediabetes

One should get a type 2 diabetes screening every one to two years if you have prediabetes.

Results indicating prediabetes are:

An A1C of **5.7–6.4%**

Fasting blood glucose of **100–125 mg/dL**

An OGTT two-hour blood glucose of **140–199 mg/d**

Chapter V

Classification of Diabetes

Until the 1960s, a systematic classification of diabetes did not exist[27]. In 1965, the inaugural World Health Organization (WHO) report on diabetes categorization was released by an Expert Committee on Diabetes Mellitus, signifying a preliminary effort towards universal consensus. . The classification was based on the age of onset and the necessity for insulin. It also recognized specific types like brittle, insulin-resistant, gestational, pancreatic, endocrine, and iatrogenic diabetes[28].

Subsequently, the National Diabetes Data Group (NDDG) formulated an updated categorization of glucose intolerance, which was endorsed by the WHO Expert Committee in 1980. The 1980 committee established two primary classifications of diabetes mellitus: insulin-dependent diabetes mellitus (IDDM), often known as type 1, and non-insulin-dependent diabetes mellitus (NIDDM), referred to as type 2.[27] The 1985 Study Group Report removed the phrases "type 1" and "type 2," but maintained the classifications IDDM and NIDDM, while including malnutrition-related diabetes mellitus (MRDM). The 1985 WHO classification relied on clinical descriptions emphasizing pharmaceutical therapy and encompassed several diabetes types, impaired glucose tolerance (IGT), and gestational diabetes mellitus (GDM).[28] It gained international acceptance as a compromise between clinical and etiological classifications, aiding clinicians in managing diabetes regardless of its origin[28].

In 1999, the WHO incorporated an approach that separated criteria based on etiology from those related to insulin deficiency or action[28]. Diabetes can progress through several clinical stages, independent of its etiology[28].

Initially used to describe diseases based on age and therapy rather than pathophysiology, the names "insulin-dependent diabetes mellitus (IDDM)" and "noninsulin-dependent diabetes mellitus (NIDDM)" have now been abolished.

[28]. Currently, the terms "Type 1" and "Type 2" are retained. According to the American Diabetes Association (ADA) 2021 classification, diabetes is classified into categories based on etiology, including Type 1 diabetes, Type 2 diabetes, gestational diabetes mellitus, and specific types of diabetes due to other causes[28].

Table 1 Etiologic Classification of Diabetes Mellitus [29]

I. Type 1 diabetes (beta-cell destruction, usually leading to absolute insulin deficiency)
 	
  1. Immune mediated
 	
  2. Idiopathic

II. Type 2 diabetes (may range from predominantly insulin resistance with relative insulin deficiency to a predominantly insulin secretory defect with insulin resistance)
III. Gestational Diabetes mellitus (GDM)
IV. Other specific types

1.   Genetic defects of beta -cell function [2]

    1. Chromosome 20q, HNF-4 alpha (MODY1)

    2. Chromosome 7p, glucokinase (MODY2)

    3. Chromosome 12q, HNF-1 alpha (MODY3)

    4. Chromosome 13q, insulin promoter factor-1 (MODY4)

    5. Chromosome 17q, HNF-1 beta (MODY5)

    6. Chromosome 2q, Neurogenic differentiation1 (MODY 6)

    7. Chromosome 9, carboxyl ester lipase (MODY 7)

    8. Transient Neonatal Diabetes (Chromosome 6p22 or 6p24, ZAC encoding zinc finger protein)

    9. Permanent Neonatal Diabetes (Chromosome 11p15, usually KCNJ11 encoding for KIR6.2 subunit of the beta-cell K_{ATP} channel)

10. Mitochondrial DNA

11. Others

2. Genetic defects in insulin action

1. Type A insulin resistance

2. Leprechaunism

3. Rabson-Mendenhall syndrome

4. Lipoatrophic diabetes

5. Others

3. Diseases of the exocrine pancreas

1. Pancreatitis

2. Trauma/pancreatectomy

3. Neoplasia

4. Cystic fibrosis

5. Hemochromatosis

6. Fibrocalculous pancreatopathy

7. Others

4. Endocrinopathies

1. Acromegaly

2. Cushing's syndrome

3. Glucagonoma

4. Pheochromocytoma

5. Hyperthyroidism

6. Somatostatinoma

7. Aldosteronoma

8. Others

5. Drug- or chemical-induced

1. Vacor

2. Pentamidine

3. Nicotinic acid

4. Glucocorticoids

5. Thyroid hormone

6. Diazoxide

7. beta-adrenergic agonists

8.   Thiazides

9.   Dilantin(phenytoin)

10. alpha-interferon

11. Others (see text)

6. Infections

    1.   Congenital rubella

    2.   Cytomegalovirus

    3.   Others

7. Uncommon forms of immune-mediated diabetes

    10.   "Stiff-man" syndrome

    11.   Anti-insulin receptor antibodies

    12.   Others

8. Other genetic syndromes sometimes associated with diabetes

    a.   Down's syndrome

    b.   Klinefelter's syndrome

    c.   Turner's syndrome

    d.   Wolfram's syndrome

    e.   Friedreich's ataxia

    f.   Huntington's chorea

g.   Laurence-Moon-Bieldel syndrome

h. Myotonic dystrophy

i.   Porphyria

j.Prader-Willisyndrome

k. Others

9.Post-transplant

Data in this table adopted from Solis Herrera -2000, NIH

Table 2 Stages of Type 1 DM [29]

	1st Stage	2nd Stage	3rd Stage
Phenotypic characteristics	-Autoimmunity -Normoglycemia Presymptomatic	-Automimmunity -Dysglycemia -Presymptomatic	-New onset Hyperglycemia -Symptomatic
Diagnostic criteria	-2 or more islet autoantibodies -No impaired	-2 or more islet autoantibodies -Dysglycemia:	-Clinical symptoms -Diabetes by standard criteria

	glucose tolerance or impaired fasting glucose	impaired fasting glucose and/or impaired glucose tolerance: FPG 100-125mg/dl and/or 2-hour plasma glucose 140-199mg/dl A1C 5.7-6.4% or a ≥10% increase in A1C	

Table 3.Classification of Diabetes:[30]

Class name	Characteristics
Insulin dependent diabetes mellitus (IDDM)	* Low or absent levels of circulating endogenous insulin and dependent on injected insulin to prevent ketosis and sustain life. * Onset predominantly in young adults but can occur at any age. * Associated with certain HLA and GAD antigens. * Abnormal immune response and cell antibodies are frequently present at diagnosis. * Etiology probably only partially, as only 35% of monozygotic twins are concordant for IDDM.
Non-insulin dependent diabetes mellitus (NIDDM)	Insulin levels may be normal, elevated, or low; hyperinsulinemia and insulin resistance.

	* Characterize most patient; insulinopenia may develop as the disease advances.
	* Not insulin-dependent or ketosis-prone under normal circumstances, but may use insulin for treatment of hyperglycemia.
	* Onset predominantly after age 40 years but can occur at any age.
	* Approximately 50% of men and 70% of women are obese
	* Etiology probably strongly genetic as 60%-90% of monozygotic twins are concordant for NIDDM
Gestational diabetes mellitus (GDM)	Glucose intolerance that has its onset or recognition during pregnancy. * Associated with elder age, obesity, family history of diabetes.

	*Conveys increased risk for the women for subsequent progression to NIDDM. * Associated with increased risk of macrosomia.

Adopted from Pradeep Singh et all 2015.

Unani classification of diabetes

1.Diabetes according to Unani classification is classified into two categories depending on how much there is sugar in the urine

A) Ziyābetus Sada, also known as Ziyābetus gair shakari, or diabetes insipidus. Excessive thirst and frequent urination are its hallmarks, yet the urine is sugar-free.

B) Ziyābetus Shakari (Diabetes mellitus), which is characterized by elevated urine sugar levels and excessive thirst and urination.

2. The signs and symptoms are further categorized into two categories based on their intensity (khiffat and shiddat).[31],[32]

A) Ziyābetus Haar: This condition causes sever acute symptoms such as increased urination and excessive thirst (polydipsia) and frequent urination (polyurea) with the symptom and sign of other *sue mizaj haar* like heat in flanks and dryness or the body, due to *sue mizaj haar sada* of kidneys

B) Ziyābetus Baarid: In which the thirst and frequency of urine is comparatively less.

Chapter VI

Clinical features of Diabetes

Signs and symptoms of diabetes are often overlooked due to the disease's chronic nature. Because the effects of high blood sugar take time to manifest, unlike many other disorders, many people do not consider it to be a significant problem. The fact that harm can start years before symptoms appear is regrettably not well known. Unfortunately, this is the case because early detection of symptoms can assist manage the disease quickly and avoid.[31]

Sign and symptoms of diabetes as per International Diabetic Federation of (IDF)[31,32] is shown in below image :

1. Unexplained weight loss
2. Frequent fatigue
3. Irritability
4. Repeated infections especially in the
   - Genital areas
   - Urinary tract
   - Skin
   - Oral cavity
   - Delayed wound healing
5. Dry mouth
6. Burning, pain, numbness on feet
7. Itching
8. Reactive hypoglycaemia
9. Acanthoses nigricans-the presence of velvety dark patches of the neck, arm pit, groin which is an indicator of insulin resistance
10. Decreased vision
11. Impotence or erectile dysfunction

Image: adopted from (Ramachandran A.2014)

Type 1 Diabetes: Sign and Symptoms of type 1 diabetes can appear abruptly, with severe hyperglycemia developing rapidly. Insulin treatment is required daily to manage the condition. The Cause of Type 1 diabetes is an autoimmune process in which the body's immune system targets the pancreatic beta-cells that produce insulin.

Type 2 Diabetes: Symptoms usually resemble those of type 1 diabetes, although with less intensity. Type 2 diabetes may be detected several years post-onset, as some individuals stay asymptomatic for an extended duration. The IDF emphasizes that early detection and management can prevent serious complications like cardiovascular disease (CVD) and diabetic foot issues

The classic symptoms of diabetes, such as frequent urination **(polyuria),** excessive thirst **(polydipsia),** and increased hunger **(polyphagia),** are common in type 1 diabetes, which rapidly develops severe high blood sugar levels. These symptoms also occur in type 2 diabetes when blood sugar levels are very high. Significant weight loss is commonly observed in type 1 diabetes or in type 2 diabetes if it remains undiagnosed for an extended period. Unexplained weight loss, tiredness, restlessness, and bodily pain are prevalent indications of undiagnosed diabetes. Mild symptoms or those that develop gradually may remain undetected..[31]

Chapter VII

Pathophysiology of Diabetes

The pathophysiology of diabetes is largely based on insulin resistance and is influenced by environmental and genetic factors. In type 1 diabetes, insulin is absent due to the autoimmune destruction of pancreatic β-cells, while in type 2 diabetes, peripheral tissues resist the effects of insulin [33,34].

Type 1 Diabetes Mellitus: The progression of type 1 diabetes depends on the rate of autoimmune destruction of pancreatic β-cells. Diabetic ketoacidosis (DKA) can occur due to rapid fat breakdown, leading to the liver processing fat into ketones and causing the blood to become acidic. Owing to the severity and advancement of type 1 diabetes mellitus, individuals become totally dependent on insulin therapy for survival. [34].

Type 2 Diabetes Mellitus: Insulin resistance and insufficiency, linked to inflammatory cytokines and increased fatty acid levels, are characteristic features of the pathogenesis of type 2 diabetes mellitus. These conditions result in increased hepatic glucose production, increased breakdown of fat, and inadequate glucose transport into target cells. Insufficiency of insulin and excessive glucagon secretion cause hyperglycemia.[33,34] Type 2 diabetes mellitus may be remain undiagnosed early on due to its slow and asymptomatic progression. Its etiology involves genetic and environmental factors, including lifestyle factors such as poor diet, age, lack of exercise, obesity, and a family history of diabetes.

Gestational Diabetes Mellitus: Gestational diabetes mellitus (GDM) is identified during the second or third trimester of gestation. Fasting and random blood glucose levels are often decreased at the commencement of pregnancy but escalate significantly during the third trimester in women with gestational diabetes mellitus.

Insulin Resistance: Insulin resistance (IR) is a condition where target tissues show a reduced response to insulin, disrupting molecular pathways[35],[36]. In order to maintain adequate glucose and lipid homeostasis, insulin resistance causes an increase in insulin secretion. Reduced glucose transport leads to a decrease in insulin-stimulated glycogen synthesis, which is the main symptom of insulin resistance in skeletal muscle. Tyrosine phosphorylation of IRS-1, which is implicated in insulin signaling, is inhibited by the accumulation of lipids in the liver and skeletal muscle.[34]

VII.1. Diagrammatic representation of pathophysiology of diabetes Mellitus type 2 (T2DM) [37]

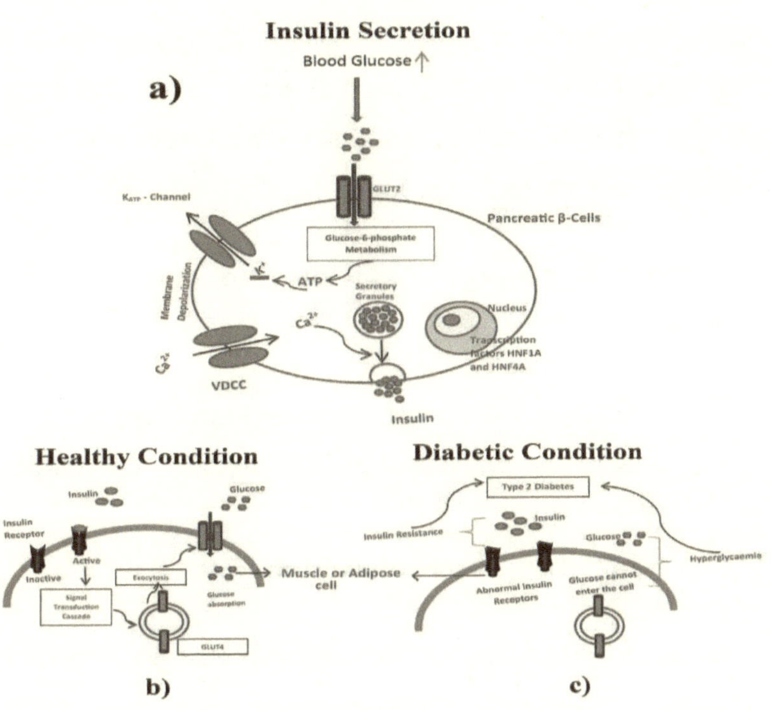

Fig.1 Diagrammatic representation of pathophysiology in type 2 diabetes mellitus (T2DM). Adopted from Internet source.

VII.2 Pathophysiology of Diabetes: Unani Concepts

The concept of *Quwa* is a distinctive aspect of *Tibb* (Unani medicine). *Quwa* refers to the inherent property of the body that enables the manifestation of life processes. These

Quwa form the foundation for various bodily functions. Every organ is equipped with a specific *Quwat* (power) that allows it to perform its designated physiological functions. These *Quwa* are unique to particular tissues or organs, ensuring the proper execution of their respective roles. The organ serves as the location for *Quwa* (faculties), and these faculties, in turn, generate functions. [38]

The *Quwa* of the body are categorized into three major divisions:

1. **Al-Quwa at-Tabi'yah (Natural Faculties)**
2. **Al-Quwa an-Nafsaniyah (Psychic or Mental Faculties)**
3. **Al-Quwa al-Haywaniyah (Vital Faculties)**

The *Al-Quwa at-Tabi'yah* are accountable for functions including ingestion, digestion, absorption, metabolism, assimilation of food, elimination of waste items, and preservation of human being. based on their functions, *Ali Ibn Abbas* classified *Quwa at-Tabi'yah* into three main faculties:

- **Quwate Ghaziyah (Nutritive Faculty)**
- **Quwate Murabbiyah (Growth Faculty)**
- **Quwate Muwallida (Reproductive Faculty)**

The **Quwate Ghaziyah (Nutritive Faculty)** is responsible for the ingestion, digestion, absorption, metabolism, assimilation of food, and elimination of waste. Based on its function, this faculty is further divided into four types of *Quwa*:

Quwate Jazibah (Power of Absorption)

This faculty enables the absorption of *Akhlat* (humors) and their movement into the cells with the assistance of various enzymes, hormones, or natural forces.

Quwate Masika (Power of Retention)

This faculty retains the *Akhlat* within the cells to facilitate *Istahalah* (metabolism).

Quwate Mughayirah (Power of Transformation)

This faculty is responsible for transforming substances, such as the phosphorylation of glucose after it enters the cells.

Quwate Dafi'ah (Power of Excretion and Propulsion)

This ability aids in the removal of waste products produced during Istahalah (metabolism) from the cells and tissues. As previously stated, every organ has a Quwat (power) that allows it to carry out specific physiological activities. The esophagus, stomach, intestines, liver, spleen, salivary glands, oral cavity, and pancreas (Banqaras) are among the organs associated in Quwate Hazima (A'zae Hazm). It claims that the liver is the primary organ of Quwate Tabi'yah.

Abu Sahl Masihi states that each of the four Quwa is found in two different places: in the liver and gastrointestinal tract and in each cell in the body. The Quwa found in bodily cells takes up nutrients and Ruh (vital energy), breaks them down and changes them into other substances, and then replaces cellular wear and tear by producing Quwat.[39], [40], [41], [42]

VII.3 Disease Review

The previously described functions of *Quwa* in *Umoore Tabi'yah* (natural principles) particularly emphasize the digestion, absorption, and transportation of nutrients from the gastrointestinal tract to tissues, as well as the absorption and retention of substances by the cells through different *Quwa*. Ancient Unani scholars (*Attibba-e-Qadeem*) did not describe the precise physiological mechanisms as modern physicians can today due to the lack of scientific advancements in their time.

With the progress of medical science, the **pathophysiology of diabetes** has been well established. The role of the **pancreas, insulin secretion, and peripheral insulin resistance** in the development of the disease has been clearly understood, along with other contributing factors to a lesser exten

Chapter VIII

Normal Insulin Physiology

Glucose homeostasis is governed by three interrelated mechanisms: hepatic glucose synthesis, glucose absorption and utilization by peripheral tissues (mostly skeletal muscle), and the influence of insulin and counter-regulatory hormones like glucagon. Insulin and glucagon have antagonistic effects on glucose homeostasis.[3]

During fasting, diminished insulin levels and elevated glucagon levels facilitate hepatic gluconeogenesis and glycogenolysis while suppressing glycogen synthesis, thus averting hypoglycemia. As a result, hepatic glucose output primarily determines fasting plasma glucose levels[43]. After food intake, insulin secretion rises while glucagon secretion decreases in response to elevated glucose levels. Insulin enhances glucose uptake and metabolism in peripheral tissues, with skeletal muscle serving as the primary site for postprandial glucose utilization. This mechanism plays a crucial role in preventing hyperglycemia and maintaining glucose balance. [26]

Insulin Biosynthesis, Secretion, and Action

Biosynthesis

Insulin is produced in the beta cells of the pancreatic islets. It is initially synthesized as an 86-amino-acid precursor polypeptide known as preproinsulin. This precursor is enzymatically processed to produce mature insulin and C-peptide, which are stored in beta-cell secretory granules and co-released upon stimulation. C-peptide functions as a dependable indicator of insulin secretion, facilitating the distinction between endogenous and exogenous insulin sources in the diagnosis of hypoglycemia. [3]

Secretion

Glucose acts as the principal regulator of insulin secretion by pancreatic beta cells; however, amino acids, ketones, other nutrients, gastrointestinal peptides, and neurotransmitters also affect this mechanism. Insulin synthesis gets started when blood glucose levels approximate 70 mg/dL, facilitated by the enhancement of protein translation and processing. [43]

Glucose enters beta cells via a facilitative glucose transporter, and its phosphorylation by glucokinase serves as the rate-limiting step in glucose-induced insulin release.

Insulin secretion follows a pulsatile pattern, characterized by small bursts every 10 minutes and larger oscillations occurring every 80–150 minutes. [26]

Incretins, released by neuroendocrine cells in the gastrointestinal tract after food intake, enhance glucose-stimulated insulin secretion and suppress glucagon release. Among them, *Glucagon-like Peptide-1 (GLP-1)* is the most potent, being secreted by L cells in the small intestine. It stimulates insulin secretion only when blood glucose levels rise above fasting levels, thereby preventing unnecessary insulin release.

Action

Upon secretion into the portal venous system, about 50% of insulin is extracted and metabolized by the liver, while the remainder enters systemic circulation and binds to insulin receptors on target tissues. The binding of insulin to its receptor activates intrinsic tyrosine kinase activity, triggering receptor autophosphorylation and recruitment of intracellular signaling molecules, such as *insulin receptor substrates (IRS)*.

These IRS proteins, along with other adaptor molecules, initiate a complex cascade of phosphorylation and dephosphorylation reactions, leading to insulin's metabolic and mitogenic effects.[26] Moreover, insulin signalling facilitates glycogen production, protein synthesis, lipid storage, and the control of several genes in insulin-responsive cells. [3]

Chapter IX

Vaccination in Diabetes

Vaccination is a vital tool in safeguarding against infectious diseases, especially for individuals living with chronic conditions such as diabetes, where immune function may be compromised. As diabetes becomes an increasingly prevalent health concern worldwide, particularly in low- and middle-income countries, the need for comprehensive care extends beyond managing blood glucose levels and preventing complications like heart disease and nerve damage. Diabetic individuals are more susceptible to infections, which can lead to more severe consequences, including hospitalization and even death. Immunization against diseases such as influenza, pneumococcal infections, and hepatitis can significantly reduce these risks. We will explore current guidelines, recommended vaccines, and the challenges of implementing vaccination programs, particularly in regions where adult immunization is not yet fully realized. By considering both global practices and local issues, this chapter aims to provide healthcare professionals with the necessary tools to integrate vaccination into the routine care of people with diabetes.

Table No.4: Vaccination in Diabetes as per American Diabetes society. [44]

Sr no.	Vaccine	Recommended ages	Schedule
1	COVID-19	Recommended for all 6 months of age and older	Current initial vaccination and boosters
2	Hepatitis B	People <60 years of People ≥60 years of age based on clinician's risk assessment	Nil
3	Influenza	Recommended for all 6 months of age and older. People ≥65 years old, there may be additional benefit from one of the high-dose inactivated or recombinant or adjuvanted inactivated influenza vaccines. The live	Annual

| | | attenuated (nasal spray) vaccine should not be used | |
| 4 | Pneumonia (older vaccine PPSV23) | 19–64 years of age | • If received PCV13, give one dose of PPSV23
• If received PCV15, follow with PPSV23 after ≥1 year
• PPSV23 is not indicated after PCV20
• Adults who received only PPSV23 may receive |

			PCV15 or PCV20 ≥1 year after their last dose
		≥65 years of age	• One dose is recommended for those who previously received PCV13 • If PCV15 was used, follow with PPSV23 ≥1 year later • PPSV23 is not indicated after PCV20
	Pneumonia (newer vaccines:	Adults 19–64 years of age, with an	One dose of PCV15 or PCV20 is

	PCV15 or PCV 20)	immunocompromising condition (e.g., chronic renal failure), cochlear implant, or cerebrospinal fluid leak	recommended by the Centers for Disease Control and Prevention (CDC)
		19–64 years of age with an immunocompromising condition	For those who have never received any pneumococcal vaccine, the CDC recommends one dose of PCV15 or PCV20
		≥ 65 years of age with an immunocomprom iseing condition have shared decision-making	• One dose of PCV15 or PCV20 • PCSV23 may be given ≥8 weeks after

		discussion with health care professionals	PCV15 • PPSV23 is not indicated after PCV20
	RSV	Older adults ≥60 years of age with diabetes appear to be a risk group	May receive a single dose of an RSV vaccine
	Tetanus, diphtheria, pertussis (Tdap)	• All adults • Pregnant individuals should have an extra dose	Booster every 10 years

Supported in part by seasonal Respiratory Illness campaign, American Diabetes Association (ADA) (Adopted from ADA)

Chapter X

Treatment of Diabetes Mellitus

The management of diabetes mellitus has undergone substantial advancements, driven by improved insights into its complex mechanisms and the growing need for effective treatment strategies. Diabetes, whether Type 1 or Type 2, is primarily defined by chronic high blood glucose levels, arising from either a lack of insulin production or insufficient insulin action. Type 1 diabetes requires lifelong insulin administration due to the autoimmune destruction of the pancreas' insulin-producing cells, while Type 2 diabetes is typically addressed through a combination of lifestyle changes, oral medications, and in more advanced cases, insulin therapy. As the prevalence of diabetes increases globally, effective treatment becomes more critical, not only to regulate blood sugar but also to prevent the onset of serious complications, including heart disease, diabetic neuropathy, and kidney failure. This chapter explores the range of treatment options available for diabetes mellitus, from traditional approaches like oral drugs and insulin to newer, innovative therapies. By analyzing current treatment guidelines, personalized care plans, and challenges in both clinical and patient settings, this chapter aims to provide healthcare professionals with a comprehensive perspective on managing diabetes and improving long-term outcomes for those affected by this chronic condition.:[45]

X.1 Oral hypoglycemic agents:

Effective care of diabetes mellitus necessitates an interprofessional strategy that incorporates lifestyle modifications, such as dietary changes and exercise, alongside pharmacological interventions tailored to achieve individualized glycemic targets. Healthcare practitioners should advocate for patients to integrate lifestyle modifications with oral pharmacological agents for optimal glycemic regulation, particularly as type 2 diabetes mellitus progresses with ongoing deterioration of pancreatic beta-cell function and insulin synthesis.

Oral Hypoglycemic Agents

- Sulfonylureas (glipizide, glyburide, gliclazide, glimepiride)
- Meglitinides (repaglinide, nateglinide)
- Biguanides (metformin)
- Thiazolidinediones (rosiglitazone, pioglitazone)
- α-Glucosidase inhibitors (acarbose, miglitol, voglibose)
- DPP-4 inhibitors (sitagliptin, saxagliptin, vildagliptin, linagliptin, alogliptin)
- SGLT2 inhibitors (dapagliflozin, canagliflozin)
- Cycloset (bromocriptine)

FDA-approved indications for the use of oral hypoglycemic agents generally pertain to type 2 diabetes mellitus.

Non-FDA approved indications

Oral hypoglycemic agents, including metformin, are utilised for the prevention of type 2 diabetes mellitus, management of gestational diabetes mellitus, treatment of polycystic ovary syndrome (PCOS) marked by menstrual irregularities, prevention of ovarian hyperstimulation syndrome in PCOS patients undergoing intracytoplasmic sperm injection (ICSI) or in vitro fertilisation (IVF), and mitigation of weight gain associated with antipsychotic medications.

Mode of Action:

Sulfonylureas

Sulfonylureas interact with adenosine triphosphate-sensitive potassium channels (K-ATP channels) located in the pancreatic beta cells. This binding obstructs these channels, altering the cell's resting membrane potential. Consequently, there is a reduction in potassium efflux, leading to an influx of calcium and the activation of insulin production.

Meglitinides

Meglitinides function via various pancreatic beta-cell receptors and complement the action of sulfonylureas. They regulate adenosine triphosphate-sensitive potassium channels in pancreatic beta cells, resulting in an increase in insulin production.

Metformin

Metformin enhances the activity of hepatic adenosine monophosphate-activated protein kinase. This action reduces hepatic gluconeogenesis and lipogenesis while enhancing insulin-mediated glucose uptake in muscles.

Thiazolidinediones

Thiazolidinediones stimulate peroxisome proliferator-activated receptor gamma (PPAR-γ), a nuclear receptor. This mechanism enhances insulin sensitivity and thus promotes peripheral glucose uptake. Moreover, it elevates the concentration of adiponectin, a cytokine released by adipose tissue that enhances the quantity of insulin-sensitive adipocytes and promotes fatty acid oxidation.

Alpha-glucosidase inhibitors

Alpha-glucosidase inhibitors competitively block alpha-glucosidase enzymes in the intestinal brush border cells. These enzymes metabolize dietary starch, and their blockage obstructs polysaccharide reabsorption and the conversion of sucrose into glucose and fructose.

DPP-4 inhibitors

DPP-4 inhibitors limit the enzyme dipeptidyl peptidase 4 (DPP-4). This inhibitor inactivates glucose-dependent insulinotropic polypeptide (GIP) and glucagon-like peptide 1 (GLP-1), among others. Thus, these inhibitors affect glucose regulation by multiple pathways, including the suppression of glucagon production, the promotion of glucose-dependent insulin release, the postponement of gastric emptying, and the increase of satiety.

SGLT2 inhibitors

SGLT2 inhibitors obstruct sodium-glucose co-transporter 2 (SGLT-2) in the proximal tubules of renal glomeruli. This inhibition obstructs over 90% of glucose reabsorption, leading to glycosuria in diabetic people, hence reducing plasma glucose levels.

Cycloset,

Cycloset, a sympatholytic dopamine D2 receptor agonist, readjusts the hypothalamic circadian rhythm potentially disrupted by obesity. This action reverses immune resistance and reduces glucose production.

Administration of oral hypoglycemic agents:

Table.5 Drug with dose for therapeutic Administration.

Name of Drug	Dose per Day
Glipizide	2.5 mg to 10 mg, taken as a single dose or in two divided doses, 30 minutes before breakfast. Maximum daily dose: 40 mg.
Glimepiride	1 mg to 4 mg, taken once a day with breakfast or twice a day with meals. Initial dose for high-risk patients: 0.5 mg daily.
Glyburide	1.25 mg to 5 mg, taken as a single dose or two divided doses.
Repaglinide	0.5 mg to 2 mg, taken in two to three divided doses per day.
Metformin	500 mg to 1000 mg, taken twice a day.
Alpha-glucosidase Inhibitors	25 mg to 100 mg, taken three times a day just before meals.

Pioglitazone	15 mg to 45 mg, taken once daily.
Rosiglitazone	2 mg to 8 mg, taken once daily.
Linagliptin	5 mg, taken once daily.
Vildagliptin	50 mg, taken once or twice weekly.
Sitagliptin	25 mg to 100 mg, taken once daily.
Saxagliptin	2.5 mg to 5 mg, taken once daily.
Canagliflozin	Initially 100 mg, increased to 300 mg, taken once daily.
Dapagliflozin	5 mg to 10 mg, taken once daily.
Empagliflozin	10 mg to 25 mg, taken once daily.
Cycloset (Bromocriptine)	Initially 0.8 mg, increased to 1.6 mg to 4.8 mg, taken once daily.

Table.6 Adverse drug reaction and contra indications of oral hypoglycemic agents:

Name of Drug	Adverse Drug Reactions	Contraindications
Sulfonylureas	Hypoglycemia, weight gain, nausea, skin rash, liver problems, cardiovascular issues	Hypersensitivity to the drug or sulfonamide derivatives, type 1 diabetes mellitus, diabetic ketoacidosis
Repaglinide	Hypoglycemia, weight gain, headache, upper respiratory tract infection, cardiovascular ischemia	Not specified
Metformin	Gastrointestinal upset (diarrhea, nausea, vomiting), lactic acidosis, vitamin B12 deficiency	Hypersensitivity to the drug, severe renal dysfunction (eGFR < 30 mL/min/1.73 m²), metabolic acidosis, diabetic ketoacidosis
Thiazolidinediones	Edema, hypoglycemia, cardiac failure, bone fracture, myalgia, sinusitis, pharyngitis	Hypersensitivity to the drug, New York Heart Association Class III or IV heart failure, serious hepatic

Name of Drug	Adverse Drug Reactions	Contraindications
		impairment, bladder cancer, history of macroscopic hematuria, pregnancy
Alpha-glucosidase Inhibitors	Flatulence, diarrhea, abdominal pain, increased serum transaminases	Hypersensitivity to acarbose, diabetic ketoacidosis, cirrhosis, inflammatory bowel disease, ulcers of the intestine, partial intestinal obstruction, digestive and absorptive issues
DPP-4 Inhibitors	Hypoglycemia, nasopharyngitis, increased serum creatinine, acute pancreatitis, acute renal failure	Dose adjustment needed for saxagliptin with eGFR < 45 mL/min/1.73 m²; sitagliptin contraindicated in patients on hemodialysis or peritoneal dialysis
SGLT-2 Inhibitors	Dyslipidemia, hyperphosphatemia, hypovolemia, fungal	History of serious hypersensitivity to the drug, end-

Name of Drug	Adverse Drug Reactions	Contraindications
	vaginosis, urinary tract infection, increased urine output, dysuria, influenza, bone fracture, renal impairment	stage renal disease (ESRD), patients on dialysis
Cycloset	Dizziness, fatigue, headache, constipation, rhinitis, nausea, weakness	Allergy to the drug, breastfeeding, syncopal migraine

Note: The contraindications and adverse reactions listed are not exhaustive and may vary based on individual patient conditions and specific formulations of the drugs. Always consult a healthcare professional for personalized advice.

Unani treatment for diabetes:

According to Unani physician correction of the temperament of kidneys and liver and restore the *Quwwate-e-Masika* (retentive power) of kidneys is crucial while treating *Ziyābetus* (diabetes Mellitus) so those drugs are used which is having these potencies.[11] [46]

Other Unani medications exhibiting hypoglycemic action have been thoroughly documented in Unani literature. Amla (*Emblica officinalis*), Anaar (*Punica granatum*), Aqaqia (*Acacia arabica*), Bel (*Aegle marmelos*), Damm-ul-akhwain (*Pterocarpus marsupium*), Elva (*Aloe barbadensis*), Gilo (*Tinospora cordifolia*), Gurmarbuti (*Gymnema sylvestre*), Jamun (*Eugenia jambolana*), Kafoor (*Cinnamomum camphora*), Kishneez (*Coriandrum sativum*), Kundur (*Boswellia serrata*), Methi (*Trigonella foenum-gracum*), Neem (*Azadirachta indica*), Tabasheer (*Bambusa arundinacea*), Sandal safaid (*Santalum album*), Mastagi (*Pistacia lentiscus*), Pakhanbed (*Bergenia ligulata*), Panbadana (*Gossypium herbaceum*), Piyaz (*Allium sativum*), Tukhm-e-kahu (*Lactuca scariola*), Tukhm-e-khurfa (*Portulaca oleracea*), Khar-e-khasak (*Tribulus terrestris*), Gul-e-mundi (*Sphaeranthus indicus*), Lokat (*Eriobotrya japonica*), Musli safaid (*Chlorophytum arundinaceum*), Juft baloot (*Quercus incana*), among others, are notable Unani single drugs purported to be efficacious.

Some compound formulations are also reported in Unani literature. *Arq-e-Gul-e-ward*, *Arq-e-kasni*, *Kushta-post-e-baiza murgh*, *Kushta khabs-ul-hadeed*, *Qurs tabasheer*, *Qurs-e-ziabetus*, *Qurs-e-kafoor* etc. some compound formulations which have also been investigated scientifically[11],[8],[47] Some single Unani drugs have been scientifically evaluated for their hypoglycemic activity in experimental models and clinical studies. Gulnar (*Punica granatum*),[48] Gilo (*Tinospora cordifolia*),[49],[50] Gurmar (*Gymnema sylvestre,*)[51]' Jamun (*Eugenia-jambolana*), Khurfa (*portulaca oleracea,*) Kishneez (*Coriandrum sativum*), Sandal Safaid (*Santalum album*), Tabasheer (*Bambusa arundinacea*), Babul (*Acacia arabica*), Damm-ul-akhwain (*Pterocarpus marsupium*)[52] are some noteworthy examples.

According to Unani physicians the drugs which altered the *Mizaj* (temperament) of kidney and liver or restore the *Quwwat-e- masika* (retention power) and *Quwwat-e-jaziba* of kidney are used to manage the disease. [47],[53], [54],[55]

Table.7 Common Marketed anti-diabetic formulations with dosage form and dose :[56]

Sr. No.	Name	Ingredients	Dosage	P/P & Ph	Manufacturer
1	Safoof-e-ziabetis	Gudmar booti, Jamun	3–6 g bid	P/P	Hermas Unani Herbal, Calicut, India
2	Cap Ziabetis	Darchini, Pan Bhadana	1–2 cap bid	P/P	Hermas Unani Herbal Pharmaceuticals, Kerala, India
3	Cap Ziyabaneel	Gunde-babool, Bark of Babool, Camphor	1–2 cap bid	P/P	Hermas Unani Herbal Pharmaceuticals, Kerala, India
4	Shakrino	Aqaqia, Tabasheer, Shilajit, Gudmar booti, Maghze-jamun, Post Anar, Post Gular, Kushta Khabsulha deed,	2 tablets bid	P/P	Rex Remedies, Delhi

Sr. No.	Name	Ingredients	Dosage	P/P & Ph	Manufacturer
		Kushta Marjan, Kushta Baize-e-murgh, Kushta Sadaf, Warq Nuqra			
5	Kalonji Sugar Powder	Kalonji powder, Tukhm-e-jamun, Gudmar booti, Tuqme-katayla, Tuqm-e-kasni, Tuqme-methi	1 tsf tid	P/P	Mohammedia Products, Karimnagar, India
6	Diabeat	Tukhm-e-kalonji, Methi seeds, Tukm-e-kasni, Neem	1–2 cap bid	P/P	Hamdard Laboratories, Gurugram, India

Sr. No.	Name	Ingredients	Dosage	P/P & Ph	Manufacturer
7	Diabetoz	Asgand, Banslochan, Chiraita, Gilo, Gudmar, Halela Zard, Kolanji, Jamun, Neem, Methi seeds, Zanjibeel	2 cap bid	P/P	Hakeem Baqai's Medicare (p) Ltd.
8	Dolabi	Gudmar-booti, Jamun, Kushta-baiza-murgh, Tukhme-hummaz, Aqaqiya, Labbabuz, Banslochan, Kushtajast, Kushta Khubsul-hadeed,	1tab bid	P/P	Hamdard Laboratories, Gurugram, India

Sr. No.	Name	Ingredients	Dosage	P/P & Ph	Manufacturer
		Gond Safaid			
9	Gurmar Capsules	Gudmar booti dried extract	1 cap bid	P/P	Dehlvi Naturals, Delhi, India
10	Jamun Sirka	Jamun fruit pulp, Water	10–15 ml/day	P/P	Dehlvi Naturals, Delhi, India
11	Kerala Capsules	Karela (bitter melon) dried extract, Karela powder	2 cap daily morning	P/P	Dehlvi Naturals, Delhi, India
12	Karelajamunras	Karela (bitter melon), Jamun	10–15 ml bid	P/P	Dehlvi Naturals, Delhi, India
13	Methi Capsules	Methi dried extract, Methi powder	2 cap bid	P/P	Dehlvi Naturals, Delhi, India

Sr. No.	Name	Ingredients	Dosage	P/P & Ph	Manufacturer
14	Qurs-Tabasheer	Tabasheer, Tukhme-khurfa, Tukhme-kahu, Gule-surkh, Gulnar, Gile-armani	5 g	Ph	Hamdard Laboratories, Gurugram, India
15	Kerala Ras	Karela (bitter melon)	10 ml bid	P/P	Dehlvi Naturals, Delhi, India
16	Qurs Ziabitis	Tukhme-khurfa, Tukhm-e-kahu, Rub-us-soos, Tabasheer, Gile-armani, Gul-e-surkh, Kishneezk husk, Aqaqia, Samag-e-arabi,	2tab bid	Ph	Dawakhana Tibbiya College, AMU, Aligarh, India

Sr. No.	Name	Ingredients	Dosage	P/P & Ph	Manufacturer
		Sandal Safaid, Sandal Surkh, Gulnar, Camphor			
17	Amla Aloe vera Kerala, Jamun juice	Amla, Gheekwar	20 ml bid	P/P	Dehlvi Naturals, Delhi
18	Qursekushta baize murgh	Kushta baize murgh, Ararot (starch)	2 tab	P/P	Dehlvi Naturals, Delhi
19	Qurse kushta zamrud	Kushta zamrud, Ararot (starch)	1 tab	P/P	Dehlvi Naturals, Delhi
20	Diab-Eaze	Gulneelofar, Methi, Karelabeej, Gilo, Jamun, Gudmar	2 cap tid	P/P	Dehlvi Naturals, Delhi

Sr. No.	Name	Ingredients	Dosage	P/P & Ph	Manufacturer
		booti, Darchini, Shilajit, Gular			
21	Qurs-e-ziyābetus khaas	Tabasheer, Satte-gilo, Maghze-khasta-e-jamun, Gurmar booti, Kushtae-baizamurgh, Kushtae-zamurrud, Loabe-asphaghol	2–3 tablets bid	Ph	Sadar Dawakhana, Delhi, India
22	Ziyābetus-C	Sandal safaid, Nishastae Gandum, Katheera, Tukhme Kahu, Gurmar booti, Chiraita	6 g powder bid	P/P	Qadari Dawakhana, Kolkata, India

Sr. No.	Name	Ingredients	Dosage	P/P & Ph	Manufacturer
		talkh, Kushta abrak, Neem, Kushta loha, Kushtae hajrul yahood, Amla, Gulnaar, Babool			
23	Diabosky	Maghaz Jamun, Gudmar Booti, Karela seed, Post Gular, Kalonji, Hulba (methi), Kushta Marjan, Shilajeet, Neem, Sat-gilo, Chiraita talk, Gond	2 pills bid	P/P	Sky Herbal Pharmacy Pvt. Ltd., Delhi, India

Sr. No.	Name	Ingredients	Dosage	P/P & Ph	Manufacturer
		Keekar (Babool)			

P/P- Patient / proprietary, PH-Pharmacopeial

Chapter XI

Complication of Diabetes

Diabetes significantly increases the threat of developing severe health issues. still, with applicable treatment and life adaptations, numerous individualities with diabetes can help or delay the onset of these complications.

Cardiovascular Disease

Cardiovascular complaint (CVD) is the primary cause of death among people with diabetes. Engaging in regular exercise and following a balanced diet can help reduce the threat of CVD and other complications[57],[58] Recent studies emphasize the significance of managing blood pressure and cholesterol situations to alleviate cardiovascular pitfalls.

Chronic Kidney Disease

Diabetes is the leading cause of Chronic kidney disease (CKD). Factors similar as genetics, blood glucose levels, and blood pressure influence the threat of developing CKD. enforcing strategies to manage these factors can help or decelerate CKD progression.

Diabetes-Affiliated Eye Disease

Diabetes is the leading cause of new cases of blindness in working- age groups and grown-ups. Regular comprehensive eye examinations are pivotal for early discovery and forestallment of vision loss. This visionary approach can significantly delay or help diabetes- related eye complaint [59]

Neuropathy

Neuropathy, or whim-whams damage, affects roughly half of all people with diabetes. Maintaining blood glucose levels within target ranges is essential for precluding or managing neuropathy. Understanding the different types of neuropathy can help identify symptoms and grease conversations with healthcare providers[60]

Foot Complications

Diabetes can lead to whim-whams damage, reduced rotation, and potentially branch loss. Regular bottom care, diabetes operation, and prompt medical discussion if issues arise can lower the threat of serious foot complications.

Skin Complications

Diabetes can impact the skin, but utmost skin conditions can be averted or treated if linked beforehand. Learning about diabetes- related skin conditions and agitating them with healthcare providers is important for effective management.

Oral Complications

People with diabetes are at an advanced threat for gingivitis and periodontitis. Maintaining good oral hygiene and regular dental checks can help or reduce the threat of complaint and other oral complications [60]

Hearing Loss

Hearing loss is more common in individuals with diabetes than in those without. For those with prediabetes, the threat is indeed advanced. Early diagnosing the signs of hair loss and taking applicable action can alleviate this issue[60]

Diabetic Ketoacidosis

Diabetic ketoacidosis (DKA) is a life-threatening condition caused by a load of ketones. Understanding the warning signs and managing blood glucose situations can help to reduce the onset of DKA[61]

Stroke

The threat of stroke is significantly advanced for people with diabetes. enforcing healthy life changes and managing blood pressure, blood glucose, and cholesterol can reduce this threat. Being apprehensive of stroke warning signs and treatments is pivotal for Prevention [58]

For the rearmost perceptivity into managing diabetes complications, recent studies punctuate the significance of comprehensive healthcare strategies, including life adaptations and regular monitoring of blood glucose and other health pointers [25]

Chapter XII

Standards of Care in Diabetes in 2025

The standards of Care council for each section creates a list of clinical questions, which are reviewed and bandied by an expert panel. In collaboration with a methodical review expert and librarian, they conduct methodical literature quests using PubMed, Medline, and EMBASE, fastening on studies published in English from June 2023 to July 2024. [62]. They also manually search journals, conference proceedings, and nonsupervisory agency websites. All applicable citations suffer a full- textbook review, and substantiation summaries are prepared with a methodologist. The summaries are reviewed by all PPC members, who make variations as demanded. Recommendations are drafted after deliberation and bear an 80 agreement for blessing.

The ADA uses a grading system to classify substantiation as A, B, C, or E, grounded on the quality of supporting substantiation. A-level substantiation comes from well-designed randomized controlled trials or meta- analyses, while E-level substantiation is grounded on expert opinion when clinical trials are impracticable or disagreeing. All recommendations are critical for comprehensive care, and their strength is grounded on the substantiation quality, not the recommendation itself. Clinicians must consider individual patient circumstances when applying these guidelines.

Table No. 8. ADA evidence-grading system for "Standards of Care in Diabetes"[26]

Level of Evidence	Description
A	Clear evidence from well-conducted, generalizable randomized controlled trials (RCTs) that are adequately powered, including: • Evidence from a well-conducted multicenter trial • Evidence from a meta-analysis that incorporated quality ratings in the analysis **Supportive evidence** from well-conducted RCTs that are adequately powered, including: • Evidence from a well-conducted trial at one or more institutions • Evidence from a meta-analysis that incorporated quality ratings in the analysis
B	Supportive evidence from well-conducted cohort studies, including:

Level of Evidence	Description
	• Evidence from a well-conducted prospective cohort study or registry • Evidence from a well-conducted meta-analysis of cohort studies **Supportive evidence** from a well-conducted case-control study
C	Supportive evidence from poorly controlled or uncontrolled studies, including: • Evidence from randomized clinical trials with one or more major or three or more minor methodological flaws that could invalidate the results • Evidence from observational studies with high potential for bias (such as case series with comparison with historical controls) • Evidence from case series or case reports **Conflicting evidence** with the weight of evidence supporting the recommendation
E	Expert consensus or clinical experience

Chapter XIII

Diet in Diabetes

Dietary management is a crucial component of diabetes care, focusing on achieving good glycemic control, maintaining ideal body weight, and addressing cardiovascular risks. Here's a summary of the key dietary principles for diabetes management, incorporating the latest recommendations:

Key Dietary Principles

Carbohydrates: The total amount of carbohydrates is more important than the source or type. Carbohydrates should contribute no more than 55-60% of daily calories. Foods with a lower glycemic index, such as whole grains, fruits, and vegetables, are recommended as they improve glycemic control and lipid parameters[63,64].

Fiber Intake: Consuming at least 14 g of fiber per 1000 kcal is advised, as it helps in reducing HbA1c levels and cardiovascular risks.

Fats: Limit fat intake to no more than 30% of daily calories, with less than 10% from saturated fats. Monounsaturated fats are preferable over saturated fats due to their beneficial effects on cholesterol levels.

Proteins: Protein intake should not exceed 20% of total energy intake. In patients with compromised renal function, protein intake may need to be reduced.

Hydration: Water is recommended over sweetened beverages, and nonnutritive sweeteners can be used in moderation to reduce calorie intake.

Individualized Plans: There is no one-size-fits-all diet for diabetes. Plans should be tailored to individual needs, preferences, and metabolic goals[63].

Recent Recommendations

The American Diabetes Association's Standards of Care in Diabetes—2025 emphasize the importance of personalized nutrition plans and highlight updates on nutrition, weight-loss medications, and technology[57].

Diet according to unani system of medicine:

Razi narrated in his book Kitab Manlayahzarah-al-tabib that if the poly urea is with the extreme polydipsia in this condition give barley water and juice of citrus fruits along with mucilage of buzre katoona. he recommended the diet should be vegetables, crud, pomegranate, resins, chickpea, and sumaq is beneficial.[58]

For quenching the thrust Maa-ush-shaier with Sharbate khaskhash, Aabe anartursh, Tursh Seeb, Tabashher, Rub Rebaas, Sharbate Zarishk are recommended.[14]

As *Tabreed wa Tarteeb is required* because the disease is mostly due to *Hararate ghariba*, following Ghizaye dawi is beneficial as diet therapy, example; *Rub Anaar, Gulnaar, Aloobukhara, Rube toot Aabe Dahi, Aabe kaddue sard, and* for diet *Hareerah* of 3 eggs which are soaked in *sirka* (Vinegar) for 24 hours. Bred prepared from husk of wheat is much recommended as it has low glycemic index.[59],[55]

↓ Ghiza (Diet):

Chicken broth, tomato broth, All type of fish and poultry meat, eggs, kidneys, Pancreas, pickles, radishes, spinach, onions, herbs, all kinds of nuts, almonds, walnuts, peanuts, sweet pumpkin seeds, seeds of Cucumber, Muskmelon, citrus dry fruits, etc., sour Foods Tea and coffee without sugar, soda water.

↓ Parheez (Dietary Restrictions):

Liver, wheat bread, rice, etc., all starchy foods, sago, arrowroot, barley, oats, sweet vegetables such as potatoes, mushrooms, turnips, all sweet fruits such as apples, pears, potatoes, grapes, oranges, apricots, dates, peaches, bananas, honey, sweets, ice cream, etc. Do not eat starchy and sugary foods. Instead of them, give more animal foods and fats. Use sugar instead of sugar.

As per recommendations of Unani physicians, drink plenty of water. In relation to the prevention of diabetes, it is said that the best foods are those that are free from sugar and starchy ingredients. Therefore, compared to non-nutritious foods, animal foods are beneficial for diabetic patients. However, since there is no choice but to eat vegetable foods, their starch should be separated and eaten using special methods. Therefore, feeding wheat bran brown bread is considered beneficial. Eggs, milk, and cheese are permitted, but it is said that it contains animal-based meat and sugary ingredients, so it should be avoided. Although milk also contains sugar, but since it is in small amounts, it can be consumed occasionally. Except for wheat bread, all types of pulses, as well as millet, and almost all cereals that contain starch are permissible.

Among fruits, sweet and sour fruits such as mangoes, grapes, raisins, apples, guavas, pears, plums, apricots, figs, mulberries, dates, etc. are prohibited. However, nuts such as almond kernels, pistachios, walnut kernels, pumpkin kernels, etc. are permitted.

Among vegetables, it is permissible to eat bitter gourd, cucumber, and fenugreek etc.

Among vegetables, spinach, Parsley, red cabbage, mustard greens, beetroot and onions are also permitted, but eating potatoes, carrots, beetroot, turnips, peas and beans is prohibited.

Tea and coffee without sugar are allowed, although some doctors allow them, but it is better to avoid them.

The patient should neither stop drinking water all at once nor should he drink it in excess.

Second idea: But the second idea is that in diabetes, since the body's essential sugar is excreted in large quantities, it is not appropriate to avoid sugar and sugar-containing products too much, otherwise there is a risk of excessive weakness and weakness.

It is also a fact that if a patient is put on a strict diet for too long, it will produce negative results instead of beneficial results, so the issue of Balanced dieting is worth considering.[55]

Chapter XIV

Perspective of Unani Physicians for Diabetes

A. Diabetes Unani Concept:

According to Syed Ismail Jurjani the basic cause of Ziyābetus is Hararat-e-kulliya due this excessive heat, kidneys absorbs water from liver and liver from mesenteries and mesenteries from stomach hence stomach is always inquest for water so the patient always feels thrusty and consume water, which excrete as it is through urine, this situation is called *Ziyābetus*. In Persian it is called *Dullab* due to similarity with pully (*charkhi*). It is also called "*Zallakul kulliya*" as it belongs to kidney and '*Zalak*' means to slip out from the lumen.

The author mentions if the disease gets chronic then it turns into or resembles like tuberculosis in context of destruction of muscle mass and fluids of the body. [12] According to Majoosi, polyurea is because of **Sue mizaj haar Gurda** due to this excessive heat in kidneys. Kidneys absorbs more liquid from blood to compensate the excessive heat, and then excrete this excess fluid to bladder which leads polyurea. Polydipsia is also there to urge the demand of fluid in body hence liver needs more fluid to maintain blood liquidity so quest for water increase. This condition is called *Ziyābetus* and *Salsalulbol.* Second cause Majoosi has mentioned that it may occur due to **sue *mizaj barid Jigar***, because of it the fluidity of bloods increases which leads to excessive absorption of water in kidneys and excreted by bladder in the form of urine which causes polyurea. All this occur due to the weakness of retention power of kidneys and increase of excretory power of kidneys.[11] According to Shaikhur Rais bu Ali Sina, Ziyābetus is like frequent urination after drinking of water, it belongs to the liquid substances. In Unani the different name of disease is *Ziyasaqoomas, Qaramees*; and in Arabic it is called as *Dawwarah, Dullab, Zallakulkulliya.* It occurs suddenly, the patient is always thirsty even after drinking water the thrust didn't resolve because of polyurea. Kidneys are not capable of retaining the water due to *Sue-mizaj Gurda*, weakness or dilatation of the organ, or the dilatation of the renal vessels. Here Ibne sina mention that it occurs due to the *Buroodat* of the whole body or liver or kidney. The other Causes are excessive cold-water consumption, or being in cold environment cause the kidneys to shrink which leads to *Ziyābetus.* Another cause is abnormal excessive heat of the kidneys with matter or without matter, to compensate it kidneys absorbs more fluid from liver and liver from other organs which leads to polydipsia and polyurea and dryness. Author opined that this disease leads towards Tuberculosis in terms of *Zubaan* (thaisis) and *Diq* (Tuberculosis) because of inadequacy of bodily fluids and dryness of organs. [8] Mohammad Azam khan mention *Ziyābetus* as, *Diabitus, Zalakulkulliya, Dullabia, Dawwarah, Parkariya, Moattisa.* The cause of Diabetes is impaired renal function or *sue mizaj jigar* or *sue mizaj badan* another cause is abnormal excess of heat in kidneys. It is said that diabetes is a chronic disease which leads towards *Zubaan* and *Diq*, and the liver become weak and general debility found in patients. [60] According to Ibne Hubalbaghdadi, narrated that *Ziyābetus* also called *Barkariya, Dullabiya, Ziyaasqoos* and *Qaramees*, and in Arabic *Zalakul-kulliya*. The cause of the disease is excessive heat of the kidneys due to which they absorb the excessive water and the quest for water arise in form of thirst, and the excessive water excretes from kidneys along with some essential bodily fluids. he added that some others had an opinion that this disease is caused due to coldness, in this type also there is sever thrust present.[14] Allama Nafees describes the disease as the renal impairment due to which the patient is always in thrust of water even after drinking plenty of water the quest for water is not satisfied and the water did not get absorb or metabolize in body it excretes as it is. This renal impairment is due to *Hararate Gurdah* (excessive morbid heat of kidneys), and kidneys are not capable of reabsorption and glomerular filtration of water hence the water descends towards the bladder and bladder excrete it frequently in form of polyurea. [59] Allama Samarqandi narrated different names of Ziyābetus like *Salsalulbool* that is polyurea; *Istisqaye anmus* meaning ascites of urinary bladder; *Dullab* means pully; *Moattesa* which means a disease of thrust for water; *Dawwarah* meaning round and round; *Barkariya* it also has the meaning same as *Dawwarah.*[55] Ziyābetus is classified as, Urdu name; Zibetus Sada and Ziyābetus shakri, Tibbi name; Ziyābetus sada, dullab and Ziyābetus shakri, Allopathic name; Diabetes Insipidus and diabetes mellitus .in Unani it is called Dullab which means rahat or charkhi that is pully.[61]

In allopathy diabetes is used for insipidus and mellitus, but commonly Diabetes is considered as diabetes mellitus.

Historically Unani and Arabic physician discuss the disease in their old text. In 17th century Wisler and in 18th century Disen and Rolo discussed their experience regarding diabetes and so on, in 1922 Benting Mekload and Jat discover insulin, which is considers as best medicine for Diabetes in Europe. [61]

Types of diabetes:

As per hakim Mohammad Azam khan there are two types of diabetes, *Ziyābetus Haar* and *Ziyābetus barid,* [60]

Types of Ziyābetus; Haar (Ziyābetus Sakri) and Baarid (Ziyābetus Sada); Ziyābetus Haar is also called *Shahidiya,*

Bol-e-Sakri, and *Bol-e-Shireen.* [55] Here Authur describes polydipsia, polyurea and persistent thrust as symptom of *Ziyābetus Sada,* and when the glycosuria is present along with this then it will be called *Ziyābetus Shakri.* [61] when the glucose present in urine temporarily it's called glycosuria, but it found persistently then it is called Ziyābetus Shakri. [61]

Types of diabetes: Ziyābetus sada and Ziyābetus shakri.

According to cause another 5 types:

1.***Ziyābetus mewi or Ghizai***; due to excess carbs in diet or intestinal dysfunction

2.***ziyābetus kibdi***; due to liver dysfunction

3.***Ziyābetus Kulwi wa Masanvi***; due to dysfunction of kidney and bladder

4.***Ziyābetus Asabi***; due to nervous system dysfunction

5.***Ziyābetus Ghuddi wa Bankarasi***; due impaired functions of ductless glands exp. Pituitary gland adrenal gland and pancreas. [61]

Causes of Diabetes:

According to Hakim Ismail Jurjani, **Ziyābetus** has 4 main causes;

1) ***Zofe kulliya*** (Renal Impairment)

2) ***Ittesaye majari-e-baul*** (Dilatation of urinary vessels)

3) *Sue mizaj haar mufrat kulliya* (altered hot temperament of kidneys)

4) *Sue mizaj barid aamma*. (altered cold temperament of whole body) Generally, Diabeties occur due *Zofe kulliya* or *sue mizaj ku*lliya or morbidity in structure of kidneys.[60] Another cause given by the author is dilatation of renal vessels due to which it is not able to retain the liquid inside. One more cause of disease is absorptive power of kidneys increases due to which it absorbs more fluid from the body and cannot be able to tolerate the load hence frequently excretion and absorption is going on. It may occur due to abnormal cold temperament of kidneys, in which the retentive power of kidneys impaired and the kidneys did not retain water in body hence there is frequent thrust to compensate the need of body for water[59].

Abnormal hot temperament of kidneys, neurological dysfunctions, excessive carbs in diet, alcoholism, drug addiction like morphine etc., some acute inflammatory diseases, sometimes physical trauma to brain and spinal cord, hereditary factors, sedentary life style, excessive cold environment, physical trauma to pancreas, psychological factors like anxiety, depression etc.[61].

The cause of disease here for Ziyābetus Sada is sue mizaj sada kulliya, or some neurological changes due to syphilis, or the malfunctioning of pituitary gland.

In case of Ziyābetus Shakri the glucose metabolism is disturbed due to dysfunction of liver and exocrine glands.[61]

Symptoms:

Symptoms of the disease is polydipsia, polyurea, and increase temperature of loin region. When the disease become chronic then the whole body becomes dry and lusterless. [14] Symptom of disease are polydipsia, polyurea, general debility, and sugar positive in urine, all this is due to imbalance diet, disturbed liver function and metabolism. The difference between Haar and baarid is in baarid only polyurea and polydipsia will be present but no sugar in urine. Allama Nafees said that "blood had sugar like juice of grape which sometimes convert in to the alcohol.

Diagnostic criteria as per unani medicine:

To rule out the cause of Ziyābetus one should check for polydipsia, hotness over loin and lumbar region along with the other symptoms of *sue mizaj haar*, but the urine is devoid of color and no burning micturition then confirm it that it's because of ***hararate kulliya.***

If the slightly reddish color urine and hotness over Rt hypochondrium then the cause of disease is ***hararate Jigar*** here it is considered, diabetes as metabolic disorder or its one of the causes is liver or metabolism or glycogenesis process.

If there are symptoms of *sue mizaj barid* along with polydipsia and general debility is present, loss of appetite and loss in power, quest for water resolves with Luke warm water or warm water and the disease convert in ascites then it's because of **Buradate kulliya.**

If its due to **Zofe gurdah** (weakness of kidneys) or **Kushadgi majari** (dilatation of renal vessels) then those symptoms of zof will be present [60]

5 Diagnostic symptoms are :1. Polyurea 2. Glycosuria 3. Polydipsia 4. Polyphagia 5. General debility[61]

Treatment:

The treatment of the disease is according to the temperament of kidneys like if *hararate kulliya* is the cause then opt for cold and nephroprotective medicine like Maa-ush-shaier with Sharbate khaskhash, Aabe anartursh, Tursh Seeb, Tabashher, Rub Rebaas, Sharbate Zarishk etc, and local application of *zimaad* (paste) of Aqaqiya, Sandal, Kasni, etc. different formulation of zimmad is given in his book. [14] The treatment of the disease is *Tabreed wa Tarteeb* because it is mostly due to *hararate ghariba*, for example; *Rub Anaar, Gulnaar, Aloobukhara, Rube toot,*

Qurs tabasheer, Qurs gulnaar, for diet *Hareerah* of 3 eggs which are soaked in *Sirka* (Vinegar) for 24 hours. The treatment was not mentioned in this book for the diabetes due to coldness, because it is very rare. [59] Razi narrated in his book *Kitab Manlayahzarah-al-tabib* that if the poly urea is with the extreme polydipsia in this condition give barly water and juice of citrus fruits along with mucilage of *buzre katoona.* he recommended the diet should be vegetables, crud, pomegranate, resins, chickpea, and *sumaq* is beneficial.

Nuskha by Raazi:
Tabasheer 10 darham, 5 dirhams of rose petals, 10 dirhams of Rab al-sous, 10 dirhams of khurfa seeds, gum arabia, white sandalwood, peeled lentils, 2 dirhams of kazbarah and 2 dirhams of sumaq soaked in vinegar, mix all the medicines and give it to the patient in the amount of 3 dirhams. keep medicines that quench thirst in the mouth, such as buttermilk (musal) taken little by little, Pomegranate seeds, Ajjas, Sumac and Ambar-baris etc.[58] another nuskha is , Boil the kernels of cotton seeds, and raisins in water and boil it till its consistency become semisolid, When it thickens, remove it and feed it in the evening. In the morning give *Sufoofe Hindi* with pomegranate water.[55]

Prognosis of disease:

Author narrated that if the disease become chronic then it affects the liver also due to which the body did not get the proper nutrition and become weak which leads towards the *Diq or Diq e Shakhukhat.* [59]. In elderly it may tolerate and but in younger than 40 years people it may lead to Diabetic coma and death. in elderly also, it leads toward pulmonary pneumonia, or tuberculosis[61]

Demographic appearance of disease:

As per hakim Mohammad Hasan Qurshi, its prevalence is more in Jews and all over the world patients of Ziyābetus are there, but more in India, Srilanka, And Italy. Age wise 40-60 years of people 48% involve while 7%of 20-40 years of age and 4% less than 20 years of age persons. In consideration of Gender male are more than females. [61]

Chapter XV

Unani antidiabetic drugs and some recent research

A. Use of herbal medicine in diabetes:

Herbal medicines have a long history of use in treating human diseases. Their anti-hyperglycemic properties can restore pancreatic cell function by enhancing insulin secretion, limiting glucose absorption, or enabling molecules in insulin-dependent activities. The World Health Organization (WHO) advocates for medicinal herbs as a principal source of healthcare according to their accessibility, cost-effectiveness, societal acceptance, and public confidence. A multitude of herbal plants are utilized worldwide in traditional healthcare systems to avoid long-term problems of diabetic mellitus (DM).[65]. Of the medicinal plants of Indian origin with antidiabetic properties, *Ficus religiosa* has bark that is used to prepare a decoction for diabetes treatment. The sitosterol-D-glucoside present in *Ficus religiosa's* bark elicits hypoglycemic effects [62].Eugenia jambolana (black plum or jamun) contains anthocyanins, glucoside, ellagic acid, isoquercetin, kaempferol, myricetin, and hydrolysable tannins. Its seeds contain jambosine and jamboline, which slow down the conversion of starch into sugar[66]. Pterocarpus marsupium has hypoglycemic, β-cell protection, and regenerative properties due to its flavonoid content, including terpenoids and phenolic compounds, such as β-sitosterol, lupenol, aurone glycosides, epicatechins, and iso-flavonoids. Epicatechins have insulinogenic properties that enhance insulin release and the conversion of proinsulin to insulin [67].While numerous medicinal plants exist, only a few have been scientifically validated, and more remain to be explored . Approximately 200 natural active substances derived from herbal plants, including polyphenols, flavonoids, triterpenes, alkaloids, and β-sitosterol, have exhibited antidiabetic properties via various mechanisms, such as regulating blood glucose levels and metabolic irregularities.[68]. Conventional medicine serves as the principal source of safe treatment for billions in developing countries. Pharmaceutical herbs and phytochemical constituents may assist in postponing the onset of diabetes mellitus complications. Every medicinal herb comprises a multitude of phytochemicals, although only a minor fraction has therapeutic efficacy. The generation of phytonutrients is influenced by the plant parts utilized, including bark, leaves, flowers, stems, fruits, and seedlings, along with the extraction methods employed..[68] For billions of people in underdeveloped nations, conventional medication is the primary source of reliable treatment. Pharmaceutical herbs and phytochemicals can potentially delay the onset of diabetes mellitus complications. Each medicinal herb contains numerous phytochemicals, but only a small percentage are therapeutically useful. The production of phytonutrients is affected by the plant parts used (e.g., bark, leaves, flowers, stems, fruits, seedlings) and the extraction methods employed.

B- Antidiabetic Unani Single drugs
Table no. 9. Illustration of single Unani drugs for diabetes

Sr.no.	Name of Drug	Scientific /English name
1	Amla	*Embelica officinalis*
2	Anar tursh	*Punica granatum*
3	Aabe-Anaar tursh	*Punica granatum*
4	Aabe dahi	Curd water
5	Aabe Kaddu	*Cucurbita moschata*
6	Aqaqia	*Acacia arebica*
7	Asgandh	*Withania somnifera*
8	Azaraqi	*Strychnos nuxvomica*
10	Bel leaves	*Aegle marmelose*
11	Chiraita	*Swartia Chirata*
12	Chhachh	Butter milk
13	Darchini	*Cinnemomum zylanicum*

16	Gilo	*Tinospora cordifolia*
17	Gule surkh	*Rosa demecena*
18	Gule mundi	*Sphaeranthus indicus*
19	Gulnaar Farsi	*Punica granatum*
20	Gurmaar booti	*Gymnema sylvestris*
21.	Hulba	*Trigonella foenum*
22.	Hummaz	*Cicerium arinetum*
23.	Jamun	*Syzigium cumini*
24.	Jawazbua (Jaiphal)	*Myristica fragrance*
25.	Jaw	*Hardeum Vulgare*
26.	Juft-e-baloot	*Quercus incana*
27.	Kafoor	*Cinnemomum camphora*
28.	Kalonji (Shoonez)	*Nigella sativa*
29.	Kasni	*Chichorium intybus*
30.	Khar-e-khasak	*Tribulus terrestris*
31.	Kishneez	*Coriandrum sativum*
32.	Kundur	*Boswellia serrata*
33.	Khashkhash	*Papaver somniferum*
34.	Karela	*Momordica charantia*
35.	Lokat	*Eriobotrya japonica*
36.	Loabe isapghol	*Plantago ovata*
37.	Maghze Tukhme Kaddu	*Curcubita moschata*
38.	Maghze khasta jamun	*Eugenia jambolica*

40.	Mastagi	*Pistacia lentiscus*
41.	Musli safaid	*Chlorophytum*
42.	Musli Siyah	*Curculigo orchioides*
43.	Naana	*Mentha arvensis*
44.	Neem	*Azadirecta indica*
45.	Pakhan bed	*Bergenia ligulate*
46.	Panmbadana	*Gossypium herbaceum*
48.	Sandal Safaid	*Santalum Album*
49.	Sandal Surkh	*Pterocarpus santalinus*
50.	Satawar	*Asparagus recemosus*
52.	Sadabahaar	*Catharanthus roseus*
53.	Sumaaq dana	*Rhus coriaria*
54.	Samaghe Arabi	*Acacia arebica*
55.	Tabasheer	*Bambusa arundinacea*
56.	Tukhme Kahu	*Lactuca scariola*
57.	Tukhme khyar	*Cucumis sativus*
58.	Tukhme Khyarzah	*Cucumis melo var utilissimus*
59.	Tukhme Khurfa	*Portulaca oleracea*
60.	Tukhme Hayat	*Withania coagulance Dunel*
61.	Tukhme Konch	*Macuna prunience*
62.	Teezpaat	*Cinnemomum Tamala*
64.	Zanjabeel	*Zijiber officinalis*

C-Details of Unani Single drugs with scientific evidence:

1. Aamla, Indian Gooseberry

Botanical name: *Emblica officinalis* Gaertn

Family: Euphorbiaceae

Mahiyat:

It is the fruit; the tree is medium-sized and the leaves are similar to those of the tamarind in tree. These fruits are green when raw, turn greenish-yellow when ripe and turn black when dried. They are about the size of a lemon. They are sour and astringent in test. They have lines (stripes) on their outer surface, from which they easily break into pieces after drying or boiling in water. When its kernel is separated, it is called Amah Munaqqa. If it is soaked in milk and dried, it will be called Sheer Amla. It is used in both fresh and dried forms. Apart from the fruit, the bark of its stem and leaves are also used medicinally.

Temperament: Cold 1 and dry 2

Actions: Cardio tonic, Brain tonic, tonic to vital organs, hepatotonic, vision enhancer (*Muqvi-e-chashm*), hemostatic, astringent, hair tonic, hair blacking agent (musavide shaar)

Chemical Analysis: Vitamin C, Iron, Fixed oil (Seed)

One kilogram of fresh Amla contains six thousand international units of Phosphatides Essential oil Vitamin C Produces

Adverse effect: constipation, colic.

Correctives: Honey, Almond Oil

Substitute: Halila Kabli

Compound formulations: Anushdaro, Jawarish Amla, Jawarish Shahi, All Itrifal.[69]

Research study: *Emblica officinalis* (Amla) seeds demonstrate notable hypoglycemic and antidiabetic effects, as evidenced by a study evaluating graded doses of aqueous seed extract in normal and streptozotocin (STZ)-induced diabetic rats. The 300 mg/kg dose emerged as the most effective, reducing fasting blood glucose (FBG) by 27.3% in normal rats and improving glucose tolerance by 25.3%–41.6% in diabetic models, comparable to the standard drug tolbutamide[70]. These effects are attributed to potential activation of pancreatic β-cells, similar to tolbutamide's mechanism, which enhances insulin secretion.

Phytochemical analysis identified flavonoids and gallic acid in the extract, with a phenolic content of 21 mg/g (gallic acid equivalent). These compounds align with known antidiabetic mechanisms observed in *E. officinalis* fruit extracts, such as enhancing insulin sensitivity, reducing oxidative stress, and modulating glucose metabolism[71]. For instance, gallic acid in Amla fruit improves glucose homeostasis via PPAR-γ activation and Glut4 translocation in adipocytes, while standardized fruit extracts reduce HbA1c and lipid levels in clinical trials[70].

2. Abe Anar Tursh, Pomegranate, Rumaan

Botanical name - *Punica granatum Linn.*

Family: Lythraceae

Mahiyat:

Pomegranate is a famous fruit whose tree is a shrub. Its flowers are funnel-shaped and orange-red in color. There are three types of pomegranate according to their taste. (1) Sweet pomegranate (2) Sour pomegranate (3) Sweet & Sour (Maikhoosh) pomegranate. All parts of pomegranate are used in medicine. Pomegranate seeds (fresh and dried), pomegranate pods, flowers (Gulnar), outer covering of pomegranate root (post bikhe anar). Pomegranate trees are found in Afghanistan (Kandahar), Iran, Iraq and India.

2.1-Anar Shireen, Sweet Pomegranate, Rumaan Halu

Temperament: Cold & wet 1 (Sard wa tar darajye awwal)

Actions: cardiotonic, Cardio enhancer and hepatoprotective, Haemopoietic

Uses: Hot flushes, heart weakness, liver weakness, anemia, its juice is used in convalescence.

Dosage: 50-100 ml

Chemical analysis: Protein, Sugar, Calcium, Phosphorus, Iron, Vit C

Adverse effect: Flatulence.

Correctives: Ginger, sour pomegranate

Substitute: pomegranate mekhush.

Compound formulation: Sharbate anar. Jawarish Anarain.

2.2 -Anar Tursh, Pomegranate sour, Rumman Hamiz

Temperament: Cold and moist 2

Actions: Qaati Safra, Asana Safra Asana Thirst -

Uses: Biliary diseases, jaundice, biliousness, nausea, vomiting, excessive thirst.

Dosage: 25-50 ml

Chemical analysis: Vit C. Tannic acid Other ingredients of sweet

Adverse effect: Harmful for those with a cold temperament.

Correctives: Ginger, Pomegranate sweet.

Alternative: Pomegranate sweet

Compound formulations: Sharbate Anar Tursh, Jawarish Anarain.

2.3- Anaar mekhuush, sweet, sour pomegranate

Mahiyat: It contains the functions and properties of both sweet and sour pomegranate.

Temperament: Cold and moist-(sour), cold 2°-(sweet)

Actions: Astringent, demulcent.

Uses: Its pulp is used in various types of diarrhea and dysentery, as a laxative.

Its decoction used as a gargle and astringent in toothache and as a laxative in Constipation. In Leucorrhoea it is used as an astringent (Mumsik). It is used in frequent urination, bleeding piles/ hemorrhoids as Sitz bath with its decoction.

Dosage: 3 - 5 grams

Chemical analysis: Tannin, Iron[69]

Research study: The aqueous extract of *Punica granatum* L.(pomegranate) demonstrates potential in improving glucose metabolism and insulin sensitivity in diabetic rats, according to a study on Alloxan-induced diabetic male Wistar rats. Researchers administered pomegranate fruit extract (PE) at doses of 100, 200, and 350 mg/kg body weight (labeled PE+Da, PE+Db, and PE+Dc, respectively) and evaluated its effects using oral glucose tolerance tests (OGTT), short-term (28.1% reduction) and long-term (67.9% reduction) treatment models. Key metabolic markers such as plasma insulin, free fatty acids (FFA), triglycerides (TG), and tissue glycogen/TG content were analyzed.[72]

Key findings include:

Gene expression modulation: Upregulation of IRS-1, Akt, Glut-2, and Glut-4 mRNA levels, enhancing glucose uptake and storage.

Metabolic improvements: Reduced fasting blood glucose (FBG), FFA, and TG levels, indicating improved insulin sensitivity and lipid metabolism.

Pancreatic β-cell function: Enhanced insulin expression and secretion, countering Alloxan-induced β-cell dysfunction.

The study suggests PE mitigates hyperglycemia and hyperlipidemia by activating insulin signaling pathways and restoring impaired glycolysis and lipolysis in diabetic rats.[73]

3. Aqaqiya, Mughliyan, Keekar, Gum Acacia, Gum Arabic

Botanical name: *Acacia arabica* Willd.

Family: Mimosaceae

Mahiyat: A famous thorny desert tree that grows up to 25 feet tall. Its leaves resemble tamarind leaves. It bears yellow flowers and greenish-white pods about the size of a palm. Acacia Extract is extract from the pods and leaves. A white or brown transparent gum oozes from the branches of the tree. Or sometimes it is released by cracking the branch. Which is called gum Arabic, this tree is found growing naturally in almost all parts of India.

Temperament: Cold and dry 2 degree

Action: Astringent, Cicatrizing, Cooling, Repellent, Hemostatic.

Uses: Tooth mobility and relaxation. Acacia bark is chewed or burned as a mouthwash or its juice is used as a poultice. The bark is used for diarrhea, premature ejaculation, impotence, discharge, gonorrhea and uterine prolapse. Its leaves are also used for gonorrhea, inflammation of the bladder and diarrhea. Its powder is astringent and astringent. A decoction of its leaves and roots is used for hemorrhoids, rectal prolapse, gonorrhea and uterine prolapse. Acacia is used for intestinal obstruction, bloody diarrhea and blood flow from all organs, and is used as a poultice in hot and humid conditions.

Dosage: 5-7 grams

Chemical analysis: Tannin, Tannin acid, Resin

Adverse Effect: Harmful to the stomach and intestines.

Correctives: Milk, ghee, oils

Substitute: Guava bark

Compound Formulation: *Sunoon-e-post Mughaliyaan, Lauq-e-nazli, Lauq-e-khashkhash, Tiryaq e Farooq.*

Dosage: 5-7grams

Chemical Analysis: Tannin is found in its leaves.

Research study: In India, Acacia arabica, also known as babul, is a traditional medicine for managing diabetic complications. Acacia arabica functions as an antidiabetic agent by acting as a secretagogue to stimulate insulin release[74]. In controlled rat studies, it induced hypoglycemia, but this effect was not observed in alloxan-induced diabetic rats. Additionally, powdered Acacia arabica seeds, when given to normal rabbits at doses of 2, 3, and 4 g/kg body weight, led to a hypoglycemic effect by promoting insulin release from pancreatic beta cells[30].

4. Asgandh: Ashwagandha, Aksan, Winter Cherry Root
Botanical name: *Withania somnifera* Dunal.
Family: Solanaceae

Mahiyat: It is a plant root which is 1-18 inches long, white-gray and smooth, the smell of fresh root is like horse urine that's why it is called Ashwa gandha; Ashwa means horse, gandha means smell which is like horse urine. it is called Nagori because it is cultivation in Nagore (Rajasthan) which is best in quality. Its plant is about one meter high, the leaves are like leaves of Adusa and the flowers are like brinjal flowers but smaller than it, in the shape of a turtle, yellowish green in color. The fruit is similar to the habbe kakanaj, mostly its root is used as medicine. It is found growing naturally almost everywhere in India, especially in UP, Delhi and Punjab. And it is also cultivated
Temperament: Hot and dry
Actions: Aphrodisiac, Nervine tonic, Semenagogue, Uterine tonic, Lactagogue, Resolvent, General tonic.

Uses: Weakness of the heart, premature ejaculation, Vaginal discharge. Its powder is used along with milk for milk production, powder is used in joint pain, gout, and menstrual bleeding. Its seeds are used to coagulate milk.

Dose: 3-5 grams

Chemical analysis: Somniferine, Alcohol, Carbohydrate

Adverse effect: For Sanguings.

Correctives: Kateera.

Substitute: White beheman.

Compound formulation: Habbe Asgandh, Majoon Muqavi Rahem, Majoon Zanjabeel, Safoo Jiryaan khas, Tiryaaq e Rahm.

Research study: *Withania somnifera*, commonly known as Ashwagandha, is traditionally used to treat various health issues, including diabetes. It has shown therapeutic potential in both animal models and diabetic patients. While withanolides are key compounds responsible for many of Ashwagandha's therapeutic effects, their role in its anti-diabetic activity has not been fully explored. This study evaluated the anti-diabetic properties of W. somnifera extracts and purified withanolides. The results showed that leaf extracts were more effective than root extracts in increasing glucose uptake in muscle and fat cells. Additionally, leaf extracts enhanced insulin secretion in pancreatic cells under basal conditions. Among the isolated withanolides, Withaferin A significantly increased glucose uptake, suggesting it contributes to Ashwagandha's anti-diabetic effects. The use of certain plant elicitors, such as methyl salicylate and chitosan, increased Withaferin A content and enhanced the anti-diabetic activity of the extracts.[75]

5. Azaraqi, Nuxvomica, Poison Nut, Kutchla, Khanaq Al-Kalb.

Botanical Name: *Strychnos nuxvomica*, Linn.

Family: Loganiaceae

Mahiyat: This is the seed of a tree fruit which is hard, round like a nut, flaky and Grayish in color and tastes very bitter. It is poisonous, so it is used as medicine after being detoxified. The tree grows up to 50 feet tall and the leaves are like mango or jamun leaves. It flowers twice in winter and spring. The fruit is the size of Bel fruit or orange. When broken, it splits into two parts and contains 2-5 seeds. Its trees are found in many cities of India, Gorakhpur, Bengal, Orissa, Bihar and Madras.

Temperament: Hot and dry 4th degree

Actions: Nerve stimulant, nerve tonic, heart stimulant, circulatory stimulant, sexual stimulant, appetizer, expectorant, phlegmatic, blood purifier, tumor remover, antidote.

Uses: Its powder and oil are used in paralysis, weakness, tremor, Leucorrhoea, joint pain and low back pain. It is used in dizziness, fainting, heart weakness, chronic cough, shortness of breath, poor appetite and gastric weakness, as a poultice in syphilis, leprosy, and uterine fibroids and plague. It tones up and stimulates the reproductive organs of the elderly by providing strength to them.

Dosage: 15 mg - 60 mg

Chemical analysis: Colubrine B, Brucine, Strychnine, Pseudo strychnine.

Adverse effect: It produces a mixture of intellect and thought process.

Correctives: Milk and ghee.

Substitute: Marking nut

Compound Formulations: *Majoon Lana, Habbe azraqi Majoon azraqi, Hab Munaish.*

Research study: Research indicates that extracts from *S. nux-vomica* seeds reduce blood glucose levels in alloxan-induced diabetic rats, a model where the toxin selectively destroys pancreatic β-cells through reactive oxygen species (ROS) generation.

In such studies, both aqueous and hydroalcoholic extracts of *S. nux-vomica* significantly lowered blood glucose levels by day 4 and 10 of treatment, outperforming the standard drug gliclazide by day 10. These effects are likely linked to phytochemicals like alkaloids, glycosides, and flavonoids, which counteract oxidative stress by enhancing antioxidant enzymes (e.g., superoxide dismutase, catalase) and reducing lipid peroxidation. Notably, the hypoglycemic action of *S.potatorum* extract appears independent of insulin secretion, instead modulating liver enzyme activity to restore metabolic balance.

Alloxan's diabetogenic mechanism involves cyclic redox reactions that generate ROS, leading to β-cell apoptosis and insulin deficiency. Despite its toxicity, alloxan remains a cost-effective agent for inducing type 1-like diabetes in rodent models. The antioxidant capacity of *S.nux-vomica* extract may mitigate this oxidative damage, offering a scientific basis for its traditional use in diabetes management. These findings highlight the potential of plant-derived compounds as alternatives to conventional antidiabetic therapies, particularly in reducing complications like hyperglycemia and diabetic ketoacidosis.[76],[77]

6.Belgiri: Bel Fruit, Urban Fruit, Bel, Indian Travel Fruit

Botanical Name*: Aegle marmelos* Corr.

Family: Rutaceae

The fruit is yellowish red and sweet in taste, fragrant and salivary. Its tree is tall, the fruit is thick, strong and heavy with hard peels, it is green when fresh, turns yellow when ripe. It is found in most parts of India.

Temperament: Cold 2 & moist 3 degree

Actions: Fresh laxative, dry Astringent, stomachic, digestive, stimulant, bark Antipyretic, leaves useful in diabetes.

Uses: Fresh bel pulp is used to relieve constipation. Its syrup is used to remove heat from the stomach and intestines. Belgiri is used in the form of syrup for various types of diarrhea, acute and chronic diseases of the stomach and all types of bleeding. Its bark decoction is useful in cough and the juice or extract of fresh leaves is useful in diabetes.

Dosage: 3 - 5 grams

Chemical Analysis: Protein, Carbohydrate, Fiber, Calcium, Phosphorus, Thiamine, Riboflavin, Gum (Galactose, arabinose), Carotene, Vit. C.

Adverse effect: Stinging, causes piles.

Correctives: Nabaat safaid.

Substitute: Ispaghol bran.

Compound formulation: *Belgri syrup, Majoon Zarab, Dawa braye ishaal, Safoof Hindi.*

Research study: In Indian medicine, *Aegle marmelos* leaf extract is used to treat diabetes. Studies have shown that a methanolic extract of *Aegle marmelos* can lower blood sugar levels in rats with alloxan-induced diabetes[78]. After continuous administration of the extract, blood sugar reduction was noticeable from the sixth day, and by the twelfth day, sugar levels decreased by 54%. These findings suggest that *Aegle marmelos* extract is effective in reducing blood glucose in alloxan-induced diabetic rats and also exhibits antioxidant activity.[78]

7.Charayita: Qasab al-Zariarah, Kali Mag (Bangla), Chiretta

Botanical Name: *Swertia chirata, Buch Ham.*

Family: Gentianaceae

Mahiyat: It is a plant that is about one meter high, the branches are round and upwardly curved, which is brown in color, the leaves are oval in shape, the flowers are small and fragrant, the plants are collected when they bloom. In terms of taste it is sweet and bitter, the bitterness is relatively less in sweet, while the bitterness is very strong in second type. Charaita sweet is more used medicinally, its plant is found in India and Iran.

Temperament: Hot & Dry 2°

Actions: Blood purifier, Antipyretic, Diaphoriac, Stomach and Liver Tonic, Appetizer, carminative, anti-helminthic.

Uses: Its decoction is use full in Leprosy, syphilis, inflammation and other Skin diseases. It is used in abdominal distension, poor appetite, indigestion, diarrhea, difficulty in micturition and seasonal fever. It increases the frequency of micturition and cure the dribbling of urine.

Dose: 5-7 grams

Chemical analysis: Chiratine, Carbonates, Rofalic Acid, Bitter substances.

Adverse effect: for kidneys

Correctives: Aneesoon

Substitute: Shahitra.

Compound formulation: *Majoon Shahitra, Arq musaffi, Jawarish Jalinoos, Roughane mujarrab.*

Research study: *Swertia chirayita* extracts, rich in bioactive compounds like swerchirin, mangiferin, and amarogentin, demonstrate significant antidiabetic potential through multiple mechanisms. These phytochemicals stimulate insulin secretion, inhibit protein glycation, and enhance insulin sensitivity in pancreatic cells, reducing hyperglycemic complications. Swerchirin, a key xanthone, lowers blood sugar in experimental models, while mangiferin combats oxidative stress and inhibits glucosidase activity, aiding in glucose regulation. Amarogentin and swertiamarin further contribute to hypoglycemic effects, with gentianine enhancing these properties. The plant's extracts also exhibit glucuronidase inhibitory activity, suggesting protective effects against diabetic complications like non-alcoholic fatty liver disease.

Studies highlight the efficacy of *Swertia chirayita's* aqueous, ethanolic, and hexane extracts in lowering blood glucose, cholesterol, and triglycerides in animal models. Hexane fractions improve insulin secretion, while ethanolic extracts outperform standard drugs like tolbutamide in some cases. Other Swertia species, such as *S.kouitchensis* and *S.mussotii*, show similar benefits via α-amylase/α-glucosidase inhibition and antioxidant activity, which may alleviate insulin resistance in type 2 diabetes. Research emphasizes optimized extraction methods to maximize bioactive compound recovery, reinforcing the plant's role as a promising candidate for managing diabetes and its metabolic complications[79]

8.Chach Chach or Chacha, buttermilk

Persian; Chach, Marathi; Taak, Gujrati; Chash, Bengali; Ghol bao majhool, Punjabi; chah / Maththa, Arebic; Moha

Mahiyat: The specific quantities of curd are put in a vessel and mixed with water and stirred with a mixer, whose other name is "raki fatha rai mahamla", until the butter comes to the top and the water that remains mixed with the ingredients of curd is the best buttermilk. The best buttermilk is the one that is made from the fresh curd of a young cow by removing all the butter. The Vedas have researched it thoroughly and have written that it is of five types: ghol, including "matha" (milk), "shota" and "chhach", the description of which is as follows.

(1) curd, including "malai", "mutha" i.e. churned curd, is called "ghol baao majhool" in Sanskrit.

(2) The curd that has been churned by removing the milk is called in Sanskrit as Muthat and, mixed with water and calm, up to the second level.

(3) Three parts of milk and one part of water are mixed with the curd that has been churned is called Takr in Hindi, Mutha, Muthat mixed with water and keep, up to the level.

(4) The curd that has been churned with equal amounts of water is called in Sanskrit as Ushoot.

(5) The curd that has been churned by adding excessive water is called Buttermilk.

Temperament: Cold and moist 2 degree.

In the book Khwarezam Shahi, it is described as cold and dry in the second level.

Properties and benefits: It increase the appetite of those with a hot temperament. And it fattens their bodies, calms the hot temper, and is useful for tuberculosis patients. It suppresses the pungency of hot poisons, quenches thirst, removes heat and inflammation of the stomach and liver. It stops bloody and bilious stools. Gargling with it mixed with honey strengthens the gums and relieves pain. It is beneficial for mouth ulcers. Heating an iron object or stone and quenching it in it is effective in stopping bilious and bloody stools. Patients with dysentery and those with a bilious temper should be given this recipe: let cow's buttermilk sit in a vessel for five to six hours so that a little sourness comes into it, then shake it well and break a third of a wheat flour bread into it and soak it. It is enough to take care of the digestion. Crush the seeds of the kharfa, soak and dry them, and then add them to the water. It reduces the thrust for days even. Doctors say that it quenches thirst in **diabetes** and other diseases. So, it is also useful for indigestion[69]. It is very useful in oral inflammation and chronic gastritis, etc., as well as in children's fever.

Research study: The use of probiotics, such as Pediococcus pentosaceus OBK05, is emerging as a promising approach for managing chronic metabolic disorders like hyperglycemia, hyperlipidemia, and cancer. Here's a breakdown of how OBK05 has shown potential in these areas:

Antidiabetic Activity[80]

In Vitro Studies: The cell-free supernatant (CFS) of OBK05 demonstrated potent antidiabetic activity by inhibiting α-amylase (72 ± 0.9%) and α-glucosidase (61 ± 0.8%) enzymes. This activity was compared to acarbose, a standard antidiabetic drug, which showed 86 ± 0.9% inhibition.

Mechanism: The inhibition of these enzymes can delay carbohydrate digestion and absorption, thereby reducing postprandial blood glucose levels.

Cholesterol-Lowering Activity

In Vivo Studies: In cholesterol-fed hypercholesterolemic mice, OBK05 intervention significantly lowered lipid levels and reduced lipid droplet accumulation in hepatocytes compared to the control group.

Mechanism: Probiotics like OBK05 can assimilate cholesterol, deconjugate bile acids, and modulate lipid metabolism, contributing to reduced cholesterol levels.

Anticancer Activity

In Vitro Studies: The CFS of OBK05 exhibited high anticancer activity against HT-29 cells (87.57 ± 1.27%) with an IC50 of 54.51 ± 1.8. FACS analysis revealed cell cycle arrest by inhibiting the G1 to S phase transition.

In Vivo Studies: In BALB/c mice models injected with HT-29 cells, oral administration of OBK05 resulted in significant histological improvements and reduced intestinal atypia.

General Probiotic Properties of OBK05

Tolerance and Adhesion: OBK05 shows tolerance to acidic pH and bile, with high adhesion efficiency to HT-29 cells, indicating its potential for gut colonization.

Antibacterial Activity: It exhibits antagonistic activity against pathogens like Pseudomonas aeruginosa and Bacillus subtilis[80]

9. Darchini: Darsini, Dalchini, Dalsini.

Botanical name: *Cinnamomum zeylanicum*, Blume.
Family: Lauraceae

Mahiyat: The fragrant bark of a tree is reddish brown in color, the taste is slightly sweet, sharp and aromatic, oil is also extracted from it, its trees are small evergreens which are mostly found in China, Ceylon and India.

Temperament: Hot, dry 2°

Dosage: 1-3 grams

Chemical Analysis: V.O. Having 48%-76% Aldehydes, Euginol

Adverse effect: Harmful to the bladder of alcoholics.

Correctives: Asaron, Kateera.

Substitute: Taj Qalami.

Compound formulation: *Jawarsh Jalinoos, Jawarsh Kamuni Kabir, Majoon-Chobchini*

Actions: cardiotonic, cardiac stimulant, tonic to vital organs, digestive, anti-inflammatory, expectorant

Oil: Rubificient, nervine-stimulant, analgesic, detergent

Uses: Cinnamon powder is used in heart diseases, palpitations, weakness of the heart, weakness of the brain, indigestion, flatulence, diarrhea, dysentery and phlegmy cough. Cinnamon oil is used in weakness of the heart and skin diseases such as scabies and leprosy.

Research study: This study aimed to explore the in vitro hypoglycemic effects of aqueous cinnamon extracts, focusing on developing a safe and soluble product for managing hyperglycemia in diabetic patients. The investigation analyzed the total phenolic content, pro-antho-cyanidins, and essential oils, which are key compounds responsible for the biological activities of cinnamon. The results indicated that Cinnamon water extracts, prepared using high pressure and decoction methods, showed the highest antidiabetic potential. Further detoxification and in-depth studies using cell cultures and experimental animals are needed to fully develop these extracts for treating diabetes mellitus.[81]

10.Gule surkh, Rose flower, Persian Rose, Rose

Botanical name: *Rosa damascena*, Mill.

Family: Rosaceae

Mahiyat: It is a beautiful and fragrant flower of a famous plant. It comes in many colors, but the original color is pink or red. It is used to make juice and perfume. The petals and seeds of the flower are used as medicine under the names of rose and rose petals.

Temperament: Cold & Dry 1°, Compound temperament

Functions: exhilarating and tonic for the heart, soothing for the nerves, soothing for the stomach and intestines.

Uses: Rose is used in the form of decoctions and for heartburn, inflammation of liver, Gastritis, uterine edema, heartburn, stomach and intestinal weakness, its extract is used in Cardiac weakness, phlegm and constipation, its Gulkand is used as a laxative, and it is used as a poultice for inflammation of liver and headache, Its distilled is used in palpitation , Anxiety, and conjunctivitis (external use), its powder is applied over the body to prevent excessive sweating and to make the body fragrant. Rose oil is massaged for ecstasy and edema, and it is used in uterine edema.

Dose: 5-7 grams

Chemical analysis: Volatile oil, Sterol, Gallic acid

Adverse effect: Harmful to the heart.

Correctives: Anise seeds.

Substitute: Benafsha, Myrrh Bakhsh.

Compound formulations*: Majoon Dabid-al-Ward, Sharbate ward mukarer.*

Research study: The inhibitory effects of extracts from *Rosa damascena* on alpha-amylase and alpha-glucosidase may alleviate side effects commonly associated with synthetic medications, including gastrointestinal disturbances. In vitro studies have shown that methanolic extracts of *Rosa damascena* exhibit a strong capacity to inhibit alpha-amylase activity, outperforming aqueous extracts and acarbose in terms of efficacy. Furthermore, in vivo experiments demonstrate that *Rosa damascena* has a dose-dependent impact on glucose levels post-meal compared to acarbose in both normal and diabetic mice.

Previous research corroborates these findings, indicating that methanolic extracts of *Rosa damascena* yield significant enzyme inhibition due to high concentrations of phenolic compounds. Other studies have also reported substantial inhibitory effects from various plant extracts on alpha-glucosidase activity, with some achieving over 75% inhibition compared to acarbose's 51%. Additionally, compounds like quercetin dihydrate have shown promising results in enhancing the inhibitory effects on alpha-glucosidase when administered alongside maltose solutions.[82]

11. Gurmar booti; Gudmar buti; Gurmar, Padpatter, Padpatram

Botanical name: *Gymnema Sylvestre*

Mahiyat: It is a small plant found abundantly in mountains of India. Its leaf's width is about two closed fingers sized and length is slightly higher than width, ovate in shape, resembles like bel (A*gel marmelos*) leaf. There is a slight bitterness in test. Its bark is more potent then leaves. Its shelf life stays many years.

Temperament: hot and dry 2nd degree

Uses: it is useful in itching, wring worm infestation, and leprosy. Nasal drop (saoot) of its juice is beneficial in sinusitis. Drinking gurmar grinded with black pepper is beneficial to the patient of cholera.

This is one of its main properties that if its leaves were chewed and then sugar, jaggary or any other sweet substance would be eaten, the test of sweet will not recognize. It is said that if some leaves of this plant put in a vessel and then add the jaggary to vessel the sweetness of jaggary will vanish totally or it become less sweet, that's why this drug is called with the name Gudmaar(sweetening killer).

If it is chewed before eating any unpleasant substant or badmazah substant the bad test will not be recognized due to its effect.

Mujarrab:

1. Hakim Najmul Ghani observed that when his friend Thakur jagannath singh ji send him some leaves and wood or branches of this plant, he chewd it in small quantity and tested the sweet substance, the sweet test become test less and when chewd in larger quantity the sweet test totally erased.

   1. Put a small amount of wine on top of a wide mouthed bottle by coating it with wood of gurmaar, Leave it for a week. After that, turn the bottle upside down and keep it safely. This infusion is very useful as antidote in quantity of 4-gram powders infusion to snake bite, opium poisoning, and patient of cholera in repeated dose.

2. In patients of plague (taoon zadah) if this drug is given the burning sensation reduces.

These two things have come in repeated experience of Maulvi Zakh Sahab, that if gurmar is combine with opium it loses its effectiveness and it eliminate the poison of an animal name Ghiraya Sakhpu, as an antidote.

Corrective: if any kind of adverse drug effect occurs then its corrective is NEEL.[69]

Research study: Gymnema Sylvester has demonstrated the ability to enhance insulin's effectiveness in lowering blood sugar levels in both type I and type II diabetes. Research indicates that the antihyperglycemic effects of dried leaf powder from Gymnema Sylvester were observed in alloxan-induced diabetic rabbits, resulting in notable changes in gluconeogenic enzyme activity and a reversal of liver damage caused during hyperglycemia. In a study involving rats, administering powdered leaves of Gymnema sylvestre at a dosage of 500 mg/kg body weight for ten days significantly mitigated hyperglycemia induced by intravenous beryllium nitrate, normalizing blood sugar levels within four days compared to ten days for untreated subjects[83].

12.Hulba: Fenugreek.

Botanical name: *Trigonilla foenum graecum, Linn.*

Family: Papilionaceae

Mahiyat: The seeds of a plant that are found in pods. These pods are about five inches long. The seeds are triangular, yellow in color, and have a bitter taste. When soaked in water, it produces mucilage. It is eaten as a culinary. It is cultivated in the gardens of India.

Temperament: Hot & dry 2

Actions: Resolvent, Demulcent, Anti-inflammatory, Painkiller, Appetizer, Lactagogue cleanser, laxative, nervine tonic, nerve stimulant.

Uses: In cough, sore throat and headache, its decoction is used along with honey. And the solution used to give benefit to remove blemishes on the face. Its mucilage is used in eye irritation, diarrhea and dysentery in the stomach and in the intestines, and in combination with salt in loss of appetite. In case of amenorrhea, its decoction is used as a drink. It is also used in cold and phlegmatic diseases such as weakness of nerves, loss of libido, joint Pain and pain in hip joint.

Dosage: 3-5 grams

Adverse effect: It is harmful to the hot temperament people.

Correctives: Barge Kasi, Pomegranate,

Substitute: Barge Hulba.

Compound formulation: *Marham Dakhalyoon, Dawa ul-Misk, Zemad Khanazir, Rogan Shifa, Qirouti Arad jau.*

Chemical composition: Alkaloids, Trigonelline, Choline, Saponin, Prolamin, F.O., V.O., Mucilage, Nicotinic acid. Vit. A, D, E, Phosphate, Lecithin, Fe, Nucleoalbumin

Research study:

Preclinical studies have identified multiple bioactive compounds in fenugreek—such as galactomannan, 4-hydroxyisoleucine (4-HIL), trigonelline, diosgenin, quercetin, and others—that demonstrate antidiabetic potential through diverse mechanisms.

Key pathways activated by these compounds include:

- Enhances phosphorylation of IRS-1, Akt, and GSK-3β while promoting GLUT4 translocation to reduce hyperglycemia.
- AMPK activation and GLP-1 modulation: Improves glucose utilization and insulin sensitivity.
- Carbohydrate enzyme inhibition: Slows glucose absorption by targeting α-amylase and α-glucosidase.
- Cellular protection: Preserves pancreatic β-cell function and mitigates oxidative stress through antioxidant activity.
- Clinical trials support fenugreek seeds' efficacy in lowering blood glucose and insulin resistance, either

alone or combined with other therapies. However, critical gaps remain:

- The exact molecular mechanisms of fenugreek extract or isolated components require deeper investigation.
- Standardized optimal dosing and treatment duration in human studies need validation to maximize therapeutic benefits.[84]

clinical trials revealed that fenugreek seed consumption significantly lowered fasting blood glucose, 2-hour postprandial glucose, and HbA1c levels in individuals with diabetes. However, substantial heterogeneity was observed across studies, primarily attributed to differences in participant diabetes profiles and variations in dosage (ranging from 5–25 g/day) and preparation formats (e.g., whole seeds, powders, or extracts).

Dose-dependent efficacy: Clinically meaningful glucose reductions occurred only with medium-to-high doses (≥5 g/day) of fenugreek seed powder, while low-dose hydro-alcoholic extracts (<2 g/day) showed no significant effects.

Acute glucose control: Postprandial glucose improvements were consistent in trials testing ≥5 g doses of powdered seeds, aligning with acute intervention studies.

Safety profile: No severe adverse effects were reported across all trials, supporting fenugreek's tolerability.[85]

13. Jamun; Maghze khasta jamun: Kalajam, Phalinda, Black Plum

Botanical name: *Eugenia jambolana*, Lam.

Family: Myrtaceae

Mahiyat: Jamun tree is evergreen. Its fruit is green and astringent when raw, similar to plum.

When ripe, it is dark purple in color, has a sweet and sour taste. The fruit (jamun), the pulp of the fruit (Maghze jamun), and the bark of the tree are used as medicine. There are many varieties of it, usually small and large. All have almost the same functions and properties. The juice of the pulp of the fruit is used to make extract(rub) and vinegar.

Temperament: Cold & Dry 2

Actions: Maghz: astringent. Jamun: Tonic for the stomach and liver, appetizer, cooling, tonic for the gums and teeth.

Uses: The pulp of the dried jamun is used alone or with other suitable medicines in the treatment of diabetes and chronic diarrhea. Jamun juice or rub-e-jamun is used in the treatment of qualitative temperamental change in stomach and liver, for anorexia, bilious and bloody diarrhea. Its bark is used in the form of a decoction and tooth powder in the treatment of hemorrhoids and toothache.

Dosage: Pulp of dried jamun: 1-3 grams, jamun juice: 20-30 ml.

Chemical analysis: Tannin, Glucoside, (Jambulin) Gallic acid, Resin, Volatile Oil (Seed) Ellagic acid, (Alk) Jambocin.

Adverse effect: Flatulence and slow digestion,

Correctives: black pepper, salt.

Substitute: One type is a substitute for another.

Compound formulation: *Jamun vinegar, Sufoof e khasta jamun, Rub-e-kabiz.*

Research study/scientific validation: This study investigates the antihyperglycemic effects and molecular mechanisms of the ethyl acetate fraction of E. jambolana seed in streptozotocin (STZ)-induced diabetic rats. The ethyl acetate fraction demonstrated antihyperglycemic activity in both short-term and long-term models, potentially due to the presence of bioactive Phyto-molecules like gallic acid and polyphenolic compounds. In the short-term, the fraction stimulated pancreatic beta-cells for insulin release, similar to Glibenclamide. Long-term treatment with the fraction led to a significant reduction in fasting blood glucose levels, recovery in serum insulin levels, and improved insulin sensitivity, possibly through increased insulin release and beta-cell regeneration. The fraction also inhibited sucrase and maltase activity in vitro, reducing postprandial blood glucose levels by interfering with dietary carbohydrate absorption. Furthermore, the study found that the fraction improved the expression of Hex-1, a key enzyme in glycolysis, and inhibited DNA degeneration in pancreatic beta-cells, suggesting its protective effects against STZ-induced apoptosis. These findings suggest that the ethyl acetate fraction of E. jambolana seed exerts its antidiabetic effects through multiple mechanisms, including insulin release, improved insulin sensitivity, inhibition of carbohydrate digestion, and protection of pancreatic beta-cells.[86]

14. Kundur: Kundur, loban, olibanum

Botanical name: *Boswellia serrata*, Roxb.

Family: Burseraceae

Mahiyat: It is an Oleo-gum-resin of a tree which is obtained by cracking the trunk in a special season. It is yellowish in the form of teardrops and has a sweetish taste. The best kind of Kundur is white on the outside and yellow inside. Its trees are found in the forests of Jhansi in India, Arabia and Africa.

Temperament: Hot and dry.

Actions: Soothing, anti-inflammatory, expectorant, phlegm-eliminating, wound-healing, astringent, memory-enhancing, moderating.

Uses: It is used in the form of powder for various types of cough, whooping cough, frequent urination, urinary incontinence, diabetes and gonorrhea. In addition, its oil is used as a massage oil for arthritis and gout, and mixed with coconut oil, as an ointment for various types of wounds, ulcers and sores.

Dosage: 1-3 grams

Chemical analysis: Essential Oil, Phytosterol, Gum, Resin

Correctives: Mushk.

Alternative: Mastagi.

Compound formulation: *Roughane Kalan, Majoon Nessian.*

Research study: Boswellia supplementation shows promise in improving both glycemic markers and lipid profiles in individuals with type 2 diabetes mellitus (T2DM). Research indicates that *Boswellia serrata* supplementation significantly reduces HbA1c levels compared to control groups, while also improving fasting blood glucose (FBG), although this improvement was not statistically significant. Furthermore, significant reductions were observed in total cholesterol (TC), triglycerides (TG), and LDL levels, alongside a slight, non-significant increase in HDL levels. These findings suggest that *Boswellia serrata* could be effective in enhancing glycemic control and improving lipid profiles in patients with T2DM[87]

15.Jaw: Shaeer; Barley; Habb

Botanical name: *Hordeolum vulgare*

Mahiyat: Barley is a famous grain.

Temperament: Cold and Dry.

Actions: Slightly astringent, Cicatrizing, detergent, Soothing, stabilizer to blood bile ratio.

Uses: Barley is less nutritious than wheat as per glycemic index. Its bread is slightly slow to digest. It is bread produces slight dryness in the body. It is fed to hot-tempered and obese people. Barley flour is used alone or with other medicines to cleanse the face and body. It is used by making sattu of barley and ashe jaw.

Special benefit: It is given to patients by making ashe jaw (Barly water) of barley.

Adverse effect: for the bladder

Correctives: Aneesoon, Gulqand

Substitute: Jawar

Compound formulation: *Tiryaq e Arba, Tiryaq e Samania.*

Barley Sattu: Barley is roasted and ground into flour. This ground flour is called Barley sattu.

Uses: Barley sattu is less nutritious than barley water (Aashe jaw). It is mostly used in summer to relieve heat and thirst. Patients also feed it to relieve hot tempers. It is used in fevers to reduce the temperature as well as a dieto-therapy. After soaking the Barley in water, straining it and sweetening it with sugar or syrup, it is a good to relieve heat and quench the thirst.

Research study: barley contains significant quantities of phenolic compounds, primarily in bound forms that remain stable during digestion.[88]n. These phenolics demonstrate glucose-lowering effects by suppressing the activity of carbohydrate-digesting enzymes α-amylase and α-glucosidase in laboratory settings. Additionally, studies using insulin-resistant liver cells show that highland barley extracts improve glucose utilization and increase glycogen storage through two key mechanisms:

Activation of the IRS-1/PI3K/Akt signaling cascade, which enhances cellular insulin sensitivity

Promotion of GLUT4 transporter mobilization to cell membranes, facilitating glucose uptake

These combined actions help stabilize blood sugar levels. The evidence supports highland barley's potential as a functional food for diabetes management, though further animal and clinical studies are needed to confirm these mechanisms in living systems[89]

16.Jawzbuwa: Jaifal

(Hindi)Jaifal; (Arabic) Jozboa; (Persian) Jozaboyad: (Sanskrut) Jatiyaphalam; (Sindhi) Jafar; (Kashmiri) Zafal; (English) Nutmeg

Botanical name: *Myristica Fragrans*

Mahiyat: It is an oval-shaped fruit similar to the areca nut, which is brownish-brown from outside and reddish inside. The smell is sharp, pleasant and fragrant, with a sweet, fragrant aroma. The nutmeg is peeled off its outer peel and is separated from it when it dries is called **Jawitri.**

Temperament: Hot and dry 2nd degree

Actions: Refreshing, Tonic to organs, aphrodisiac, reduces halitosis, carminative, stomachic.

Uses: Its oil is extracted and used as a poultice along with tonic medicines. It is applied as a poultice for headaches, joint pain and paralysis.

It is mixed with sesame oil and massaged in paralysis, weakness and joint pain etc.

Adverse effect: For lungs and liver

Correctives: Coriander and honey.

Substitute: Jawitri and balchhad.

Dosage: ½ masha - 1 masha

Chemical analysis has revealed the following components in nutmeg and bisbasa (Jawitri). Fusarium oil, Proteins, Fat, Starch, Salivary substance.

By pressing the nutmeg, an oil is obtained which is called Butter of Nutmeg. It contains myrcene and myristic acid and the rest is oil.

Compound formulations: *Jawarish Ood Shireen, Habbe A'saab, Ma'ujun Choobchini bisbasa, Jawarish Bisbasa, Jawarsh Zaraoni.*

Research study: Key findings Research study shows in vivo effect as, the combination therapy significantly reduced fasting blood glucose levels in both alloxan- and glucose-induced hyperglycemic mice compared to glimepiride alone, demonstrating a time-dependent improvement.

Statistical analysis (Student's t-test) confirmed the efficacy of the combined treatment in lowering blood glucose.

Computational Insights

Molecular docking revealed glimepiride had a binding affinity of −7.6 kcal/mol with sulfonylurea receptor 1, while macelignan (a compound from nutmeg) showed stronger interactions with peroxisome proliferator-activated receptors (PPARs): −9.2 kcal/mol with PPARα and −8.3 kcal/mol with PPARγ.[90]

Molecular dynamics simulations indicated macelignan-PPARα/γ complexes exhibited greater stability than pioglitazone-PPAR complexes, suggesting enhanced therapeutic potential.

Comparative Efficacy

The nutmeg-glimepiride combination outperformed the glimepiride-pioglitazone pairing in computational stability assessments, highlighting its potential as a novel antidiabetic strategy.[91]

17. Mastagi: Mastagi, Mastagi Roomi, Alaq, Kundur Roomi,

Botanical name: *Pistacia lentiscus* Linn. (Anacardaceae)

Mahiyat: It is a resinous substance that is extracted from a tree by cracking or exuding it spontaneously. It is white, yellowish, transparent, in the shape of teardrops and has a slightly sweet, aromatic taste. Its tree is small and evergreen. The best mastic is cultivated in the islands of Rome. It is imported into India.

Temperament: Hot & dry 2 degree.

Actions: Stomach and liver tonic, anti-inflammatory, astringent, expectorant, moisture-absorbing, astringent.

Uses: Mustagi leaves are used in weakness of stomach and liver, diarrhea, flatulence, indigestion, cough and shortness of breath. In addition, it is also used to clean and strengthen teeth and remove halitosis.

Dosage: 1-3 grams

Chemical analysis: E.O., Resin, Starch, Acid, Carbohydrates.

Adverse effect: Harmful for bladder diseases.

correctives: Soak in grape vinegar.

Substitute: Turmeric, Izkhar Makki.

Compound formulations: Jawarish Mastagi, Jawarish Jalinoos, Jawarish Tabasheer.

Botanical name: *Pistacia lentiscus*

Research findings: Inhibition of α-glucosidase and α-amylase is a significant strategy in the management of Type

2 Diabetes (T2D), as it reduces glucose production and absorption after meals. These enzymes play a crucial role in carbohydrate digestion, with α-amylase initiating the process in the mouth and continuing in the small intestine, while α-glucosidase further breaks down oligosaccharides into absorbable glucose.

Enzymatic Roles and Inhibition Mechanisms

α-Amylase (E.C. 3.2.1.1) and α-glucosidase (E.C. 3.2.1.20) are key targets for antidiabetic therapies. Inhibiting these enzymes can lead to decreased postprandial hyperglycemia by slowing down carbohydrate digestion and delaying glucose uptake into the bloodstream. Common synthetic inhibitors such as acarbose, voglibose, and miglitol are used clinically but often come with side effects like gastrointestinal discomfort

18. Pudina: Fudanj, Naana, Mint

Botanical name: *Mentha arvensis,* Linn.

Family: Melastomaceae

Mahiyat: It is a fragrant plant. Usually this plant grows up to one foot tall. From it, the essence (sat) is obtained, which is called menthol. These plants are found in India, Japan and China. There are different types of it in terms of its native and characteristics, but all of them have almost the same functions and properties.

1)Mentha longifolia (Peppermint, Pudina Barri)

2). Mentha spicata (Garden mint, pudina Bustani)

3) Mentha piperata (Peppermin, Pudina Filfili)

4) Mentha aquatica (River mint, Pudina Nahri)

5) Mentha pulegiu (Mushktaramashi)

6) Mentha arvensis (Mountain mint, Pudina Kohi)

Temperament: Hot & Dry 2nd degree

Actions: digestive, Carminative, antiseptic, diuretic, Painkiller, anti-inflammatory, antidote, diaphoretic, Absorbent, Rubefacient, anti-helminthic.

Uses: In the form of decoction or powder, it is used in stomach diseases, abdominal pain, flatulence, vomiting, nausea, diarrhea and jaundice. Drinking its decoction or inhaling it kills intestinal worms. Its decoction is used to eliminate worms of nose and ear. To remove blemishes on the face, it is mixed with vinegar and apply. It is grounded powder use to apply on the affected area of a rat bite etc., it absorbs the poison and provides relief in pain. It works well for amenorrhea and retention of urine.

Dosage: 3 - 5 grams.

Chemical analysis: Penthitine, Volatile Oil, Menthol, Acetic Acid:

Adverse effect: Harmful to the intestines.

Correctives: Kateera.

Substitute: One type of another.

Compound formulation: *Jawarish Pudina, Jawarish Anarain, Arq, Ajeeb.*

Research study: Mentha arvensis has been traditionally used for its antidiabetic, anticarcinogenic, antiallergic, antifungal, and antibacterial properties. Research has focused on the phytochemical analysis and pharmacological potential of Mentha arvensis for drug discovery, using both in silico and in vitro methods. The Mentha arvensis extract may have antioxidant and anti-inflammatory effects, which may be due to its polyphenolic properties.[92]

19.Pambadana:

Cotton Seed, Silk Cotton Seed, Habbul qatan, tukhme banola, Tukhme Kapaas

Botanical name: *Gossypium herbaceum*, Linn.

Family: Malvaceae

Description: It is the seed of the cotton plant, the pulp of which is used as medicine, its plants are 3 to 5 Feet long, the edges of the leaves are split in three to seven places, the flowers are sour and red and purple in color, its fruits (pods) are conical in shape, inside which there is cotton, each pod separated from the cotton contains 5-7 seeds, its plant is found in India, Pakistan, Egypt and America.

Temperament: Hot and moist 2 degree

Actions: Aphrodisiac, Semenogouge, lactagaouge, a purgative of phlegm, detergent, diuretic.

Uses: Its syrup or juice is used in weight loss, general debility, loss of libido, hypo lactation weakness, Azoospermia, cough, acute and subacute nephritis. The powder is used to remove facial blemishes.

Dosage: 3 - 5 grams

Chemical analysis: Protein: Globulins, Amino acids, Carbohydrate Raffinose, Minerals: Ca, P, K, Na, Mg, Mng, Fe, Cu, S. Vitamins: B. Complex Vit. A, D, E. Glucoside: Quercimeritrin.

Adverse effect: for the kidneys.

Correctives: Banafsha.

Substitute: Tukhme kurtum.

Compound formulations: *Majoon Arad khurma, Majoon Pumbadana.*

Research study: Alloxan induces diabetes by generating reactive oxygen species, leading to the destruction of pancreatic β-cells and elevated blood glucose levels. The findings indicated that diabetic rats exhibited reduced body weight and elevated blood sugar compared to normal rats. However, administration of ethyl ether and ethanol extracts of Gossypium herbaceum significantly lowered blood glucose levels, potentially by enhancing insulin secretion from existing β-cells or through mechanisms independent of insulin, such as inhibiting glucose production or absorption. Additionally, the extracts improved lipid profiles by reducing total cholesterol (TC), triglycerides (TG), low-density lipoprotein (LDL), and very low-density lipoprotein (VLDL), while increasing high-density lipoprotein (HDL), which is cardioprotective. The presence of bioactive compounds like flavonoids, saponins, and phenolic compounds in the extracts likely contributes to these beneficial effects. Overall, Gossypium herbaceum shows promise for managing diabetes and associated lipid abnormalities, highlighting the need for further research to isolate active compounds and understand their mechanisms of action.[93]

20.1. Sandal: White sandalwood, Sandalwood, Sandal Wood

Botanical name: *Santalum album*, Linn.

Family: Santalaceae

Mahiyat: White sandalwood is a relatively small tree, the inner wood of the tree trunk is quite fragrant, this wood is used as medicine under the name of white sandalwood. Both red and white sandalwood are collectively called Sandalain and are generally used together. Oil is also extracted from it. Its trees are found in Bangalore, Mysore and other parts of South India in India.

Temperament: Cold 3rd & dry 2nd degree

Actions: Cardiotonic, disinfectant, expectorant, blood purifier.

Uses: White sandalwood is used in the form of a Majoon or powder for heart weakness, heartburn, toxemia, urinary tract infection, gonorrhea, chronic cough. Sandalwood oil is used in tablets or capsules for gonorrhea, prostatitis, dysuria and cystitis. It is also very useful in cough and bronchitis.

Dosage: 3-5 grams, Oil: 5-7 drops

Chemical analysis: Santalol (Essential oil), Tannic acid

Adverse effect: loss of libido.

Correctives: Honey.

Substitute: Camphor, Ushna

Compound formulation: *Dawaul misk moatadil), Khamira Sandal, Jawarish Tabasheer*

20.2. Sandal Surkh: Red sandal wood, Lalchadan, Raktachandan.

Botanical name: *Pterocarpus santalinus* linn.

Mahiyat: Its tree is10 to15 meter heighted, its outer covering is blackish white colored, on incision, dark red colored exudate ooze out. its wood is of dark red color and having pleasant smell, used as medicine and called Red Sandal wood.

Temperament: cold and dry 2nd degree

Action: Astringent, blood purifier, refrigerant, painkiller, diaphoretic, refreshing and heart tonic.

Uses: In the case of diarrhea, excessive sweating, hematuria, hypermenorrhea, hemoptysis, fever, blood purifier. For clearing the breath, its infusion or decoction is best.

Dosage: 3-5 grams

Chemical analysis: Santaline. Glucoside, Coloring matter

Adverse effect: loss of libido.

Correctives: Honey

Substitute: white sandalwood, camphor, Ushna

Compound formulation: *Habbe suzak, arq e Suzak (Roughan).*

Research study: The treatment with the petroleum ether fraction of Santalum album did not result in a significant reduction in blood glucose levels during the Oral Glucose Tolerance Test (OGTT). However, after a prolonged treatment period of 60 days, there was a notable decrease in blood glucose levels. Glycated hemoglobin (HbA1c), which is known to rise in diabetes mellitus patients, showed a significant reduction in diabetic rats treated with this extract, indicating improved glycemic control. Interestingly, there was no significant increase in insulin levels when compared to the diabetic control group or those treated with metformin.

Diabetes mellitus often leads to severe complications such as arteriosclerosis affecting renal, peripheral, and cardiovascular vessels. Alterations in serum lipid profiles are common in diabetes and heighten the risk of coronary heart disease. The study found that a dosage of 10 µg/kg body weight of the extract significantly lowered blood glucose, total cholesterol (TC), triglycerides (TG), and low-density lipoprotein (LDL) levels while increasing high-density lipoprotein (HDL) levels after 60 days. This improvement suggests a reduced risk of coronary events.

Excessive lipid metabolism can lead to decreased insulin-stimulated glucose uptake and insulin resistance. The findings indicated that Santalum album extract effectively improved lipid profiles and reduced the atherogenic index—a marker of cardiovascular risk—more effectively than metformin. The atherogenic index decreased from 267% to 139% in the treatment group compared to a reduction from 267% to 222% in the metformin group.

The high-performance liquid chromatography (HPLC) analysis of the extract revealed a major peak likely corresponding to α-santalol and β-santalol, which comprise about 90% of the oil fraction. In summary, Santalum album petroleum ether fraction at a low concentration of 10 µg/kg body weight can significantly enhance lipid profiles in diabetic rats, demonstrating potential advantages over metformin for cardiovascular health. Although immediate blood glucose reduction was not observed, prolonged treatment appears beneficial for glycemic control and preventing insulin resistance through lipid-lowering actions.[94]

21.Tabasheer Bamboo Manna

Botanical name: *Bambusa arundinans* Willd.

Family: Gramineae

Mahiyat: It is an exudate that oozes from the cavities and knots of bamboo, which is found in the form of white and blue crystal. Due to its blue color, it is called Tabasheer Kabud. This fluid is milky white and thin when fresh, but when dried, it takes the form of crystals. Bamboo trees are found in abundance in the Terai regions of North India and the foothills of the Himalayas.

Nowadays it is produced artificially and is the most available.

Temperament: Cold and dry 2nd degree

Actions: Astringent, Cardiotonic, anti-acid, anti-fungal, anti-bacterial, Hepatotonic, cooling, cicatrizing.

Uses: Medicinally, it is used in the form of powder for heart weakness, Palpitation, febrile illness, tuberculosis. typhoid fever, measles and smallpox, ulcers, Diarrhea, piles, gastric reflux and acidity.

It is used in powder or paste form for burn and scald.

Dosage: 1-3 grams

Chemical analysis: Silica 90%, Peroxide of Iron, Potash Calcium, Aluminum, choline, Betain, Nuclease, Urease, Oxalic acid, Benzoic acid, Reducing sugar, Resin, Wax.

Adverse effect: Produces obstruction (Sudda).

Correctives: Oils and fat

Substitute: Sumaq, Khurfa

Compound formulation: *Qurs Tabasheer kafoori, Safofe Sat gilo.*

Research study: The exudate from the node of this plant has been utilized in Persian medicine for the treatment of diabetes. It demonstrates inhibitory efficacy against α-amylase and α-glucosidase enzymes, along with hypoglycemic effects through enhancement of serum insulin and regeneration of pancreatic tissue and Langerhans islets. The exudate exhibited a notable decrease in glucose-6-phosphatase and fructose-1,6-bisphosphatase, along with a reduction in HbA1c (glycated hemoglobin), total cholesterol, and triglycerides in streptozotocin-induced diabetes. The leaves exhibit antidiabetic properties by enhancing antioxidant function and facilitating the regeneration of Langerhans islets, pancreatic tissue, hepatocytes, and renal glomeruli and tubules. b- Sitosterol glucoside and stigmasterol are recognized substances associated with this pharmacological effect. [83]

22. Sumaq dana Sumaq Sumach

Botanical name: *Rhus coriaria, Linn.*

Family: Anacardiual

Mahiyat: This is the thin skin of the fruit of a small tree. The fruits are the size of lentils and grow in clusters. There is a very thin red skin on top of these fruits which easily becomes round. It is called the *poste sumaq* or *gard sumac*. Its taste is slightly sour and flavorful. Its tree is 2-3 meters high. Its leaves are reddish long and have toothed edges. Its trees are found in Spain, Italy, Iran and Afghanistan.

Temperament: Cold Dry 2°

Action: Depressant, astringent, decongestant, stomachic, bile reducing (*Taqlile safra*).

 Uses: Sumaq is used in various types of diarrhea, bilious diarrhea, dysentery, constipation, vomiting, intoxication, thirst, weakness of the stomach, blood flow, excessive urination and excessive menstruation. Its paste is used as a gargle for toothache and to strengthen it, and its leaves are used as a poultice for various types of ulcers and hemorrhages.

Dosage: 3-5 grams

Chemical analysis: Tannin, Fixed oil.

Adverse effect: Harmful to the liver.

Correctives: Mastagi

Substitute: Zarishk.

Compound formulation: *Anushdaro sada.*

Research study: Studies have shown that *Rhus coriaria* possesses antidiabetic properties. The hydroalcoholic extract of its seeds and ethanolic extract of its fruits have been found to reduce blood glucose levels in diabetic models. The extracts also improve lipid profiles by increasing HDL and decreasing LDL cholesterol levels Mechanism of action the antihyperglycemic effects may be related to the inhibition of carbohydrate digestion or absorption, possibly through the inhibition of alpha-amylase and alpha-glucosidase activities.

Rhus coriaria extracts exhibit antioxidant properties, which can help prevent complications associated with diabetes by enhancing antioxidant enzyme activities like superoxide dismutase (SOD) and catalase (CAT).[95]

23. Tukhme Kaahu:

Botanical name: *Lactuca sativa,* Linn.

Family: Compositae

Mahiyat: Its plant is approximate 1 meter in hight, found in both wild and cultivated (dashti aur bustani). Leaves of cultivated variety is used as vegetable, the fruit is like opium poppy, when an incision is given on outer surface of poppy it oozes, this latex is called "opium of kaahu" inside this fruit, mall khaki or white colored sticky seeds are found, which have a mucilaginous taste, there are many types of kaahu, oil is extracted from it. The grass called khas is a different plant which is sometimes misidentified with kahu.

Temperament, Seed: Cold-dry, leaf: Cold and moist 2

Actions: Cooling, pain-relieving, hypnotic, narcotic, bile-reducing and thirst-quenching, antispasmodic.

Uses: Seed is used in the form of juice (sheerah) in madness, melancholy, insomnia, headache, bilious fever, hemorrhagic fevers and intense thirst. It is applied to the forehead in hot headaches and insomnia. Leaf is very useful for people with bilious and hemorrhagic temperaments and is also used in hot cough, itching, madness, melancholy, jaundice, gonorrhea and retention of urine. Oil is used in massage and nasal drops in headaches.

Dosage: 3-5 grams

Chemical analysis: Volatile Oil, Resin, Potassium, Calcium, Vit E, Oxalic acid, Lactucopiorin.

Adverse effect: loss of libido

Corrective: Mastagi.

Substitute: Poppy seeds.

Compound formulations: *Roughan Labube Saba'a, Qurse musalas, Qurse tabasheer kafoori.*[69]

Research findings: *Lactuca scariola* (prickly lettuce), a common green leafy vegetable in North Karnataka, is traditionally used for its antidiabetic properties. Research has focused on evaluating the hypoglycemic effects of aqueous extracts from *L. scariola* leaves, examining both in vivo and in vitro scenarios, with and without the presence of nickel (II), at pH levels of 7.0 and 9.0. The methods involved determining the percentage of glucose reduction using the glucose oxidase-peroxidase enzymatic method at specified pH levels and a UV-Vis spectrophotometer. Hypoglycemic activities were assessed in alloxan-induced diabetic male rats under acute and sub chronic exposure conditions[96]. Results indicated significant changes in the λ max value of Ni (II) when combined with *L. scariola* extracts at both pH levels, along with a notable reduction in glucose concentration, even with the presence of Ni (II) in vitro. Furthermore, both acute and sub chronic supplementation of *L. scariola* leaves led to improved glucose tolerance and blood sugar regulation in diabetic rats, regardless of nickel (II) treatments. These findings suggest that *L. scariola* could serve as a substitute for synthetic drugs in treating diabetic patients[96]

24. Tukhme Hayat: Paneer phool

(Urdu)Paneer; (Punjabi)Paneer dodi; (Sinidhi) Peer Band; (Farsi) Paneer baad;(Pahadi naam)Kham zeerah; (Latin) Wtihamus; (Hindi) Akri;(Sindhi) Panier Bin [97]

Botanical name: *Withania coagulance*

Mahiyat: Withania Coaglans are the seeds of a small shrub which is a type of Withania. These seeds are round like cats but slightly larger and have a white covering like a juice. Inside the covering, there are several single laced pages that are glued to each other. The taste is slightly bitter, sour and sour in smell.

Temperament: Hot and dry 2nd degree

Habitat: Kohat. Dera Ghazi Khan. Peshawar (Rahd Province) Sindh and Blochistan –

Actions and uses of the seeds - Carminative, tonic to stomach and Mughaliz are seeds. Soak one or two seeds in water and extract the juice and feed them to infants. Indigestion, stomach pain is relieved. Tie four or five seeds in a bag and boil them in half a glass of cold milk or rub them in water or milk and add them to the milk. In half an hour, high-quality curd is prepared.

If there is stomach pain, feeding a few seeds with lukewarm water immediately provides relief. The milk made from these seeds (mixed with sugar) is used to treat menstrual cramps and uterine bleeding. The active ingredient of these seeds is a yeast substance that is very similar to animal cheese.

Research study: *Withania coagulans* has been extensively studied for its potential antidiabetic properties. Withanolide-A, isolated from the n-hexane fraction of W. coagulans, has been evaluated for its anti-diabetic activity through enzyme inhibitory activity[98]. Coagulans fruits has shown potential in preventing diabetes by inhibiting α-glycosidase and α-amylase enzymes, which play a crucial role in glucose metabolism.

Phytochemical screening of the hydroalcoholic extract of *W. Coagulans* fruits revealed significant inhibition of α-glucosidase activity, which helps in delaying the peak blood glucose level. Aqueous extracts of *W. coagulans* have been found to contain trace minerals like calcium and magnesium, contributing to their hypoglycemic effects. Additionally, the aqueous extract of *W. Coagulans* flowers improved insulin sensitivity and reduced blood glucose levels in rats with type 2 diabetes.

Hydroalcoholic extracts of *W. Coagulans* dried fruits demonstrated antidiabetic and antihyperlipidemic activities in diabetic rats. Methanolic extracts of *W. Coagulans* fruits contain significant amounts of total phenols, flavonoids, and alkaloids, contributing to their antimicrobial and antidiabetic properties. Ethanolic extracts of *W. coagulans* fruits have also shown hypoglycemic effects in diabetic rats.

Furthermore, *W. coagulans* fruit aqueous extracts have been shown to reduce nicotinamide and insulin-related enzyme activity. Novel withanolides like coagulanolide, along with other identified withanolides from *W. coagulans* fruits, have exhibited antihyperglycemic actions. Aqueous extracts of *W. coagulans* fruits have reduced blood glucose levels in both normal and diabetic rats[98].

The use of nanotechnology to deliver *W. coagulans* extracts has shown promise in mitigating diabetes-related complications by combining anti-diabetic and anti-inflammatory properties. Overall, *W.coagulans* demonstrates significant potential as a natural remedy for managing diabetes due to its diverse bioactive compounds and their effects on glucose metabolism.[99]

25. Zanjabeel; Sonth, Adrak, Shrang Veer, Ginger

Botanical name: *Zingiber officinalis,* Rosc.

Family: Zingiberaceae

Mahiyat: This is the underground stem (Rhizome) of the plant, which is greenish or yellowish in color when fresh, has a sharp taste and is bitter when cooked. In the fresh state, it is called *Adrak* and when it turns brown after drying, it is called zanjabeel or Sonth. It is of two types, fibrous and non-fibrous, found in most parts of India, UP, Gujarat, Punjab and Madras.

Temperament: Hot and dry 3rd degree.

Actions: Digestive, carminative, astringent, stimulant and tonic to nerves, aphrodisiac, anti-phlegmatic, anthelminthic, astringent

Uses: Ginger is used in the form of powder for indigestion, flatulence, poor appetite, it is useful in hyperacidity, intestinal worms, phlegmatic disease, asthma, cough, paralysis, nausea and weakness of sexual power. Fresh ginger extract is also used in all the above diseases. Juice of ginger boiled in an oil is beneficial for use as a massage for rheumatic pain, backache, joint pain, joint pain and gout.

Dosage: 1-2 grams

Chemical analysis: Gingerin, Gingerol, Resin, Oil, Potassium: Chemical Analysis Oxalate, E.O. (Camphene, B Phellandrene & Zingiberene)

Adverse effect: Harmful to hot temperament.

Corrective: Almond oil

Substitute: (Dare filfil) Peppermint.

Compound formulation: *Sufoof e hazim, Majoon zanjabeel, Jawarish kamooni.*

Research study: The study examined how *Zingiber officinale* Roscoe (ginger) rhizome extract influences glucose uptake mechanisms in L6 skeletal muscle cells, focusing on its potential antidiabetic effects. Researchers treated L6 myotubes with varying concentrations of ginger extract, metformin (2 mM), insulin (200 nM), or troglitazone (20 µM) for 24 hours, followed by a 10-minute 2-[^{3}H]-deoxy-D-glucose (2-DG) uptake assay. They analyzed GLUT1 and GLUT4 transporter protein and mRNA levels to identify activation pathways.

The study revealed that ginger extract enhances glucose uptake: Ginger extract at 400 µg/ml increased glucose absorption by 208.03% ± 10.65 compared to baseline.

Pathway inhibition: This effect was blocked by inhibitors of protein synthesis (3.5 µM cycloheximide), PI3 kinase (1 µM wortmannin), and mTOR (15nM rapamycin), indicating dependence on these pathways.

GLUT1 upregulation: Ginger extract elevated GLUT1 protein expression by 1.6-fold at 4 hours, 2.03-fold at 8 hours, and 2.25-fold at 24 hours. Similarly, GLUT1 mRNA levels increased progressively, peaking at 2.32-fold after 8 hours.

The study concluded that ginger enhances glucose transport primarily by stimulating GLUT1 expression through PI3-Kinase and AMPK activation, rather than GLUT4. These mechanistic insights support ginger's potential role in managing hyperglycemia.

D. Unani single Drugs not recommended for diabetes in Unani literature but possess antidiabetic activity

Table no. 10. Unani single Drugs not recommended for diabetes in Unani literature but possess antidiabetic activity

Sr. no.	Name of drug	Scientific name	Ref.
1	Maghz Khasta-e-Anb	*Mangifera indica L.*	[100]
2	Post e Kekar	*Acacia arabica L.*	[101]
3	Satavar	*Asparagus racemosus Willd*	[102]
4	Waj Turki	*Acorus calamus L.*	[103]
5	Sibr	*Aloe vera L.*	[104]
6	Khulanjaan	*Alpinia galangal (L.) Willd*	[105]
7	Sharifa	*Annona squamosa L*	[106]
8	Fufal	*Areca Catechu L.*	[107]
9	Brahmi	*Bacopa monnieri L*	[108]
10	Khardal	*Brassica nigra L.*	[109]
11	Gul-e-Teesu	*Butea monosperma lam*	[110]
12	Habbul Qilqil	*Cardiospermum halicacabum L.*	[111]
13	Beikh Kibr	*Capparis spinosa L.*	[112]
14	Zera Siyah	*Carum carvi L.*	[113]
15	Sazaj Hindi	*Cinnamomum tamala Nees*	[114]
16	Daar Chini	*Cinnamomum verum J. S. Presl*	[115]
17	Zafran	*Crocus sativa L.*	[116]

18	Amaltas	*Cassia fistula L.*	[117]
19	Kasni	*Cichorium intybus L.*	[118]
20	Muqil	*Commiphora mukul hook ex stocks*	[119]
21	Zard Chob	*Curcuma longa L. rhizomes*	[120]
22	Shoneez	*Nigella sativa L.*	[121]
23	Gul-e-Nilofar	*Nymphaea stellata Willd*	[122]
24	Khurfa Siyah	*Portulaca oleracea L.*	[123]
25	Bed Injeer	*Ricinus communis L*	[124]
26	Anabus Salab	*Solanum nigrum L.*	[125]
27	Balela	*Terminalia belerica Roxb*	[126]
28	Halela	*Terminalia chebula Retz*	[127]
29	Biskhapra	*Trianthema portulacastrum L.*	[128]
30	Asgandh	*Withania somnifera (L.) Dunal*	[129]

Chapter XVI

Future Implication of this Book

1. Enhanced Integrative Treatment Approaches

Increased Collaboration: The book could encourage greater collaboration between conventional medical practitioners and Unani medicine specialists. This could lead to the development of integrative treatment plans that combine the strengths of both systems, potentially leading to more effective and personalized diabetes management.

Holistic Patient Care: By highlighting the holistic principles of Unani medicine (diet, lifestyle, herbal remedies), the book may inspire healthcare providers to adopt a more comprehensive approach to patient care, addressing not just blood sugar levels but also overall well-being.

Personalized Medicine: Unani medicine's focus on individual humoral balance could contribute to the development of personalized treatment strategies tailored to a patient's specific needs and constitution.

2.Further Research and Validation

Stimulation of Scientific Inquiry: The book could spark further scientific research into the efficacy and mechanisms of action of Unani medicines for diabetes. This could involve clinical trials, pharmacological studies, and investigations into the active compounds in traditional herbal formulations.

Evidence-Based Practice: As more research emerges, it could lead to the development of evidence-based guidelines for the use of Unani medicine in diabetes management, ensuring safe and effective application.

Drug Discovery: The book may highlight potential new drug candidates from Unani herbal remedies, prompting further investigation and possible development of novel pharmaceuticals.

3.Public Health Impact

Increased Awareness and Access: The book could raise public awareness about Unani medicine as a complementary or alternative approach to diabetes management, potentially increasing access to these therapies.

Preventive Strategies: Unani medicine's emphasis on lifestyle and dietary modifications could contribute to the development of effective preventive strategies for diabetes, particularly in high-risk populations.

Reduced Healthcare Burden: If Unani medicine proves to be effective in managing diabetes, it could potentially reduce the burden on conventional healthcare systems by providing affordable and accessible treatment options.

4.Educational Advancements

Curriculum Development: The book may influence medical and Unani education by incorporating integrative approaches to diabetes management into the curriculum.

Training Programs: It could lead to the development of specialized training programs for healthcare professionals interested in integrating Unani medicine into their practice.

Knowledge Dissemination: The book can serve as a valuable resource for students, researchers, and practitioners, facilitating the dissemination of knowledge about Unani medicine and its potential role in diabetes care.

5. Policy and Regulation

Integration into Healthcare Systems: Increased evidence of the effectiveness of Unani medicine could prompt policymakers to consider its integration into national healthcare systems.

Regulation of Unani Practices: The book may contribute to the development of regulations and quality control standards for Unani medicine practices, ensuring patient safety and efficacy.

Funding for Research: It could encourage government and private organizations to allocate funding for research into Unani medicine and its potential benefits for public health.

By exploring the potential of Unani medicine in addressing diabetes, this book has the potential to make positive changes in the lives of countless people around the world.

Bibliography:

1. JL L. The Gale Encyclopedia of Alternative medicine. 2nd Edition. Farmington Hills USA: Gale Group; 2005.

2. Edwaeds C, Toft A, Walker B. Davidson's Principal and Practice of Medicine. 19th Edition. New York: Churchill Livingstone; 2004.

3. Jameson JL, Kasper DL, Longo DL, Fauci AS, Hauser SL, Loscalzo J. Diabetes mellitus: Diagnosis, classification, and pathophysiology. Harrisons Princ Intern Med Online McGraw-Hill Educ 2018;

4. Becker K, Ronald C. Principal and Practice of Endocrinology and Metabolism. 3rd ed. New York: lippincott, William's and Willkins Publisher; 2002.

5. David H, Herbert LD. Kelley's Textbook of internal medicine. 4th ed. New York: lippincott, William's and Willkins Publisher; 2000.

6. Sapra A, Bhandari P. Diabetes [Internet]. In: StatPearls. Treasure Island (FL): StatPearls Publishing; 2025 [cited 2025 Mar 9]. Available from: http://www.ncbi.nlm.nih.gov/books/NBK551501/

7. διαβαίνω [Internet]. billmounce.com [cited 2025 Mar 9];Available from: https://www.billmounce.com/greek-dictionary/diabaino

8. Ibne S. Al-Qanoon Fil-Tib. NM Ed New Delhi Idarae Kitabul Shifa 2007;

9. Sina I. Al Qanoon fit tib (Urdu translation by Kantoori GH). New Delhi: Idara Kitabus Shifa; 2009.

10. Khan MA. Haziq. 1st ed. New Delhi: Jamia Humdard; 1408.

11. Majoosi A bin A. Kamil-us-sana (Urdu translation by Hkm. Ghulam Hussain Kantoori). Idara Kitab-Us-Shifa New Delhi India 2010;

12. Ismail J. Zakheera Khwarzam Shahi (Urdu Translation by Hakeem Hadi Husain Khan). Vol VI., New Dehli: Idara Kitabu sh Shifa; 2010.

13. Zohar I. Kitabut Taiseer (Urdu translation by Khan HH). New Delhi: CCRUM; 1986.

14. Baghdadi A. Kltab-Almukhtarat Fit-Tib (Urdu translation by CCRUM). New Delhi: CCRUM; 2004.

15. Razi A. Al Hawi Fil Tib. Vol IX. New Delhi: CCRUM; 2001.

16. Gilman AG. Goodman & Gillman's The pharmacological Basis Of Therapeutics. 10th Edition. New York: McGraw-Hill; 2001.

17. Eknoyan G, Nagy J. A history of diabetes mellitus or how a disease of the kidneys evolved into a kidney disease. Adv Chronic Kidney Dis 2005;12(2):223–9.

18. South-East Asia diabetes report 2000 — 2045 [Internet]. [cited 2025 Mar 10];Available from: https://diabetesatlas.org/data/en/region/7/sea.html

19. Pradeepa R, Mohan V. Epidemiology of type 2 diabetes in India. Indian J Ophthalmol [Internet] 2021 [cited 2025 Feb 28];69(11):2932–8. Available from: https://www.ncbi.nlm.nih.gov/pmc/articles/PMC8725109/

20. Frontiers | Prevalence, Awareness, Treatment and Control of Diabetes in India From the Countrywide National NCD Monitoring Survey [Internet]. [cited 2025 Feb28];https://www.frontiersin.org/journals/public-health/articles/10.3389/fpubh.2022.748157/full

21. Lancet study: More than 100 million people in India diabetic [Internet]. 2023 [cited 2025 Feb 28];Available from: https://www.bbc.com/news/world-asia-india-65852551

22. Exploring Diabetes Epidemic in India | India Science, Technology & Innovation - ISTI Portal [Internet]. [cited 2025 Feb 28];Available from: https://www.indiascienceandtechnology.gov.in/featured-science/exploring-diabetes-epidemic-india

23. Ramachandran A, Snehalatha C. Current scenario of diabetes in India. J Diabetes [Internet] 2009 [cited 2025 Feb 28];1(1):18–28. Available from: https://onlinelibrary.wiley.com/doi/abs/10.1111/j.1753-0407.2008.00004.x

24. Mathur P, Leburu S, Kulothungan V. Prevalence, Awareness, Treatment and Control of Diabetes in India From the Countrywide National NCD Monitoring Survey. Front Public Health [Internet] 2022 [cited 2025 Feb 28];10. Available from: https://www.frontiersin.org/journals/public-health/articles/10.3389/fpubh.2022.748157/full

25. Schlesinger S, Neuenschwander M, Barbaresko J, Lang A, Maalmi H, Rathmann W, et al. Prediabetes and risk of mortality, diabetes-related complications and comorbidities: umbrella review of meta-analyses of prospective studies. Diabetologia [Internet] 2022 [cited 2025 Mar 4];65(2):275–85. Available from: https://www.ncbi.nlm.nih.gov/pmc/articles/PMC8741660/

26. Diabetes Diagnosis & Tests | ADA [Internet]. [cited 2025 Feb 27];Available from: https://diabetes.org/about-diabetes/diagnosis

27. Sreenivasamurthy L. Evolution in Diagnosis and Classification of Diabetes. J Diabetes Mellit [Internet]

2021 [cited 2025 Feb 15];11(5):200–7. Available from: https://www.scirp.org/journal/paperinformation?paperi d=113164

28. Sreenivasamurthy L. Evolution in Diagnosis and Classification of Diabetes. J Diabetes Mellit [Internet] 2021 [cited 2025 Feb 15];11(05):200–7. Available from: https://www.scirp.org/journal/doi.aspx?doi=10.4236/jd m.2021.115017

29. Solis-Herrera C, Triplitt C, Reasner C, DeFronzo RA, Cersosimo E. Classification of Diabetes Mellitus [Internet]. In: Feingold KR, Anawalt B, Blackman MR, Boyce A, Chrousos G, Corpas E, et al., editors. Endotext. South Dartmouth (MA): MDText.com, Inc.; 2000 [cited 2025 Feb 15]. Available from: http://www.ncbi.nlm.nih.gov/books/NBK279119/

30. Singh P, Mishra A, Singh P, Goswami S, Singh A, Tiwari KD. Diabetes mellitus and use of medicinal plants for its treatment. Indian J Res Pharm Biotechnol 2015;3(5):351.

31. Ramachandran A. Know the signs and symptoms of diabetes. Indian J Med Res [Internet] 2014 [cited 2025 Mar 5];140(5):579–81. Available from: https://www.ncbi.nlm.nih.gov/pmc/articles/PMC43113 08/

32. Pathan S, Piemonte L, Malanda B, Savuleac R. IDF Executive Office - Belgium.

33. What Is Insulin Resistance? [Internet]. Clevel. Clin. [cited 2025 Feb 15];Available from: https://my.clevelandclinic.org/health/diseases/22206- insulin-resistance

34. Savage DB, Petersen KF, Shulman GI. Mechanisms of Insulin Resistance in Humans and Possible Links With

Inflammation. Hypertension [Internet] 2005 [cited 2025 Feb 15];45(5):828–33. Available from: https://www.ahajournals.org/doi/10.1161/01.hyp.0000 163475.04421.e4

35. Li M, Chi X, Wang Y, Setrerrahmane S, Xie W, Xu H. Trends in insulin resistance: insights into mechanisms and therapeutic strategy. Signal Transduct Target Ther [Internet] 2022 [cited 2025 Feb 15];7(1):1–25. Available from: https://www.nature.com/articles/s41392-022-01073-0

36. Zhao X, An X, Yang C, Sun W, Ji H, Lian F. The crucial role and mechanism of insulin resistance in metabolic disease. Front Endocrinol [Internet] 2023 [cited 2025 Feb 15];14. Available from: https://www.frontiersin.org/journals/endocrinology/arti cles/10.3389/fendo.2023.1149239/full

37. Diagrammatic-representation-of-pathophysiology-in-type-2-diabetes-mellitus-T2DM.png (850×918) [Internet]. [cited 2025 Feb 28];Available from: https://www.researchgate.net/profile/Prasad-Vss-2/publication/327981958/figure/fig1/AS:67758218595 9424@1538559590413/Diagrammatic-representation-of-pathophysiology-in-type-2-diabetes-mellitus-T2DM.png

38. Haleem A M. Mufradate azeezi. New Delhi: CCRUM; 2009.

39. Maseehi A. Kitabul Miya Fit Tib (Urdu translation by CCRUM). New Delhi: CCRUM; 2008.

40. Kirmani N. Kulliyate Nafeesi(Urdu translation by kabeeruddin). New Delhi: Idara Kitabus Shifa; YNM.

41. Ahmad S. Introduction to Al Umur Attabiyah. 1st ed. New Delhi: Saini Printers; 1980.

42. Azmi A. Concept of Uani Mwdicine. 1st ed. New Delhi: Jamia Humdard; 1995.

43. DeFronzo RA, Ferrannini E, Groop L, Henry RR, Herman WH, Holst JJ, et al. Type 2 diabetes mellitus. Nat Rev Dis Primer [Internet] 2015 [cited 2025 Mar 3];1(1):1–22. Available from: https://www.nature.com/articles/nrdp201519

44. Diabetes and Vaccinations | American Diabetes Association [Internet]. [cited 2025 Feb 26];Available from: https://professional.diabetes.org/clinical-support/vaccinations

45. Ganesan K, Rana MBM, Sultan S. Oral Hypoglycemic Medications [Internet]. In: StatPearls. Treasure Island (FL): StatPearls Publishing; 2025 [cited 2025 Mar 1]. Available from: http://www.ncbi.nlm.nih.gov/books/NBK482386/

46. Huble I. Kitab al Mukhtarat Fit Tib(Urdu translation By CCRUM). New Delhi: CCRUM; 2005.

47. Ahmad F. Classification of Unani drugs. Delhi: Maktab eshatul quran; 2005.

48. Jafri MA, Aslam M, Javed K, Singh S. Effect of Punica granatum Linn.(flowers) on blood glucose level in normal and alloxan-induced diabetic rats. J Ethnopharmacol [Internet] 2000 [cited 2025 Mar 9];70(3):309–14. Available from: https://www.sciencedirect.com/science/article/pii/S03 78874199001701

49. Khanal P, Patil BM, Mandar BK, Dey YN, Duyu T. Network pharmacology-based assessment to elucidate the molecular mechanism of anti-diabetic action of Tinospora cordifolia. Clin Phytoscience [Internet] 2019 [cited 2025 Mar 9];5(1):35. Available from:

https://clinphytoscience.springeropen.com/articles/10.1186/s40816-019-0131-1

50. Patel MB, Mishra S. Hypoglycemic activity of alkaloidal fraction of Tinospora cordifolia. Phytomedicine [Internet] 2011 [cited 2025 Mar 9];18(12):1045–52. Available from: https://www.sciencedirect.com/science/article/pii/S09 44711311001 53X

51. Gaytán Martínez LA, Sánchez-Ruiz LA, Zuñiga LY, González-Ortiz M, Martínez-Abundis E. Effect of Gymnema sylvestre Administration on Glycemic Control, Insulin Secretion, and Insulin Sensitivity in Patients with Impaired Glucose Tolerance. J Med Food [Internet] 2021 [cited 2025 Mar 9];24(1):28–32. Available from: https://www.liebertpub.com/doi/10.1089/jmf.2020.002 4

52. Vijayan D, Sibi G. Pterocarpus marsupium for the treatment of diabetes and other disorders. J Comp Med Alt Healthc [Internet] 2019 [cited 2025 Mar 9];9(1):555754. Available from: https://www.academia.edu/download/116046696/JC MAH.MS.ID.555754.pdf

53. Kabeeruddin M. Al Akseer. Publisher: New Delhi: Ejaz Publishing House; 2003.

54. Jeelani G. Makhxane Hikmat. Lahore: Matba Nawal Kishor Steem Press; 1910.

55. Kabeeruddin M. Sharah Asbab. First. New Delhi: Idara Kitabus Shifa; 2009.

56. Hamiduddin M, Ali W, Jahangeer G, Al A. Unani formulations for management of diabetes: An overview. Int J Green Pharm [Internet] 2018 [cited 2025 Mar 6];12(4):S769–83. Available from:

https://www.researchgate.net/profile/Gazi-Rather/publication/330936957_Unani_formulations_for_management_of_diabetes_An_overview/links/5c5c7902a6fdccb608af36d3/Unani-formulations-for-management-of-diabetes-An-overview.pdf

57. Lower Your Risk of Diabetes Complications | ADA [Internet]. [cited 2025 Mar 4];Available from: https://diabetes.org/about-diabetes/complications

58. Raazi AMBZ. Kitab Man la Yahzarah Al tabeeb (Urdu Translation by mohammad Sajid, Mohammad Arshad Jamal Bilal Ahmad). 1st ed. New Delhi: Hidayat publishers and Distributors ,Okhla,;

59. Qurshi A. Moalijaate Nafeesi (Urdu translation by Lakhnawi MA). New delhi: Idara Kitabus Shifa; 2022.

60. Khan MA. Akseer-e-Azam. Urdu Transl Hkm Kabeeruddin Idara Kitab Us Shifa New Delhi 2011;22:705–9.

61. Qurshi H. Jame-ul-HikHmat. New Delhi: Idara Kitabus Shifa; 2011.

62. Singh TG, Sharma R, Kaur A, Dhiman S, Singh R. Evaluation of renoprotective potential of Ficus religiosa in attenuation of diabetic nephropathy in rats. Obes Med 2020;19:100268.

63. Minari TP, Tácito LHB, Yugar LBT, Ferreira-Melo SE, Manzano CF, Pires AC, et al. Nutritional Strategies for the Management of Type 2 Diabetes Mellitus: A Narrative Review. Nutrients [Internet] 2023 [cited 2025 Mar 5];15(24):5096. Available from: https://www.ncbi.nlm.nih.gov/pmc/articles/PMC10746081/

64. Yeh YK, Yen F, Hwu C. Diet and exercise are a fundamental part of comprehensive care for type 2

diabetes. J Diabetes Investig [Internet] 2023 [cited 2025 Mar 5];14(8):936–9. Available from: https://www.ncbi.nlm.nih.gov/pmc/articles/PMC10360 374/

65. Katiyar D, Singh V, Gilani SJ, Goel R, Grover P, Vats A. Hypoglycemic herbs and their polyherbal formulations: a comprehensive review. Med Chem Res 2015;24(1):1–21.

66. Rizvi SI, Mishra N. Traditional Indian medicines used for the management of diabetes mellitus. J Diabetes Res 2013;2013(1):712092.

67. Xu F, Wu H, Wang X, Yang Y, Wang Y, Qian H, et al. RP-HPLC characterization of lupenone and β-sitosterol in Rhizoma Musae and evaluation of the anti-diabetic activity of lupenone in diabetic Sprague-Dawley rats. Molecules 2014;19(9):14114–27.

68. Mukherjee PK, Maiti K, Mukherjee K, Houghton PJ. Leads from Indian medicinal plants with hypoglycemic potentials. J Ethnopharmacol 2006;106(1):1–28.

69. Ghani N. Khazayanul Advia. New Delhi Idarae Kitabul Shifa 2010;1121–2.

70. Majeed M, Mundkur L, Paulose S, Nagabhushanam K. Novel Emblica officinalis extract containing β-glucogallin vs. metformin: a randomized, open-label, comparative efficacy study in newly diagnosed type 2 diabetes mellitus patients with dyslipidemia. Food Funct [Internet] 2022 [cited 2025 Mar 11];13(18):9523–31. Available from: https://pubs.rsc.org/en/content/articlelanding/2022/fo/ d2fo01862d

71. Variya BC, Bakrania AK, Patel SS. Antidiabetic potential of gallic acid from Emblica officinalis: Improved glucose transporters and insulin sensitivity

through PPAR-γ and Akt signaling. Phytomedicine Int J Phytother Phytopharm 2020;73:152906.

72. Parmar HS, Kar A. Antidiabetic potential of Citrus sinensis and Punica granatum peel extracts in alloxan treated male mice. Biofactors [Internet] 2007 [cited 2025 Mar 11];31(1):17–24. Available from: https://content.iospress.com/articles/biofactors/bio00967

73. Huang TH, Peng G, Kota BP, Li GQ, Yamahara J, Roufogalis BD, et al. Anti-diabetic action of Punica granatum flower extract: activation of PPAR-γ and identification of an active component. Toxicol Appl Pharmacol [Internet] 2005 [cited 2025 Mar 11];207(2):160–9. Available from: https://www.sciencedirect.com/science/article/pii/S0041008X04005769

74. Modak M, Dixit P, Londhe J, Ghaskadbi S, Devasagayam TPA. Indian herbs and herbal drugs used for the treatment of diabetes. J Clin Biochem Nutr 2007;40(3):163–73.

75. Gorelick J, Rosenberg R, Smotrich A, Hanuš L, Bernstein N. Hypoglycemic activity of withanolides and elicitated Withania somnifera. Phytochemistry [Internet] 2015 [cited 2025 Feb 26];116:283–9. Available from: https://www.sciencedirect.com/science/article/pii/S0031942215000953

76. Bhati R, Singh A, Saharan VA, Ram V, Bhandari A. Strychnos nux-vomica seeds: Pharmacognostical standardization, extraction, and antidiabetic activity. J Ayurveda Integr Med [Internet] 2012 [cited 2025 Mar 11];3(2):80. Available from: https://pmc.ncbi.nlm.nih.gov/articles/PMC3371563/

77. Preparation of non-toxic dosage of aqueous extract of Strychnine alkaloid from the stem pieces of Strychnos-nux- vomica plant for the controlling of blood sugar level in Diabetes induced rabbits - ProQuest [Internet]. [cited 2025 Mar 11];Available from: https://www.proquest.com/openview/977e034066ad8 43c21bfc75d3b5e5f17/1?pq-origsite=gscholar&cbl=54977

78. Sabu M, Kuttan R. Antidiabetic activity of Aegle marmelos and its relationship with its antioxidant properties. Indian J Physiol Pharmacol 2004;48(1):81–8.

79. Dey P, Singh J, Suluvoy JK, Dilip KJ, Nayak J. Utilization of Swertia chirayita Plant Extracts for Management of Diabetes and Associated Disorders: Present Status, Future Prospects and Limitations. Nat Prod Bioprospecting [Internet] 2020 [cited 2025 Feb 20];10(6):431–43. Available from: https://doi.org/10.1007/s13659-020-00277-7

80. Bhukya KK, Bhukya B. Exploration of Antidiabetic, Cholesterol-Lowering, and Anticancer Upshot of Probiotic Bacterium Pediococcus pentosaceus OBK05 Strain of Buttermilk. Probiotics Antimicrob Proteins [Internet] 2023 [cited 2025 Mar 12];15(6):1484–500. Available from: https://link.springer.com/10.1007/s12602-022-10002-0

81. Wariyapperuma WANM, Kannangara S, Wijayasinghe YS, Subramanium S, Jayawardena B. In vitro anti-diabetic effects and phytochemical profiling of novel varieties of Cinnamomum zeylanicum (L.) extracts. PeerJ [Internet] 2020 [cited 2025 Feb 26];8:e10070. Available from: https://peerj.com/articles/10070

82. Alsalti AA, Hasan N, Aldia D. IN-VITRO AND IN-VIVO HYPOGLYCEMIC EFFICACY OF ROSA DAMASCENA PETALS EXTRACTS. Bull Pharm Sci Assiut Univ [Internet] 2022 [cited 2025 Feb 20];45(2):593–604. Available from: https://bpsa.journals.ekb.eg/article_271532.html

83. Omoirri M, Odigie O, Gbagbeke K, Ajegi I, Oseyomon J, Okafoanyali O, et al. A Review on Ethno-pharmacology of Antidiabetic Plants. Asian Plant Res J 2018;1(1):1–22.

84. Antidiabetic potential of fenugreek (Trigonella foenum-graecum): A magic herb for diabetes mellitus - Sarker - 2024 - Food Science & Nutrition - Wiley Online Library [Internet]. [cited 2025 Mar 12];Available from: https://onlinelibrary.wiley.com/doi/full/10.1002/fsn3.44 40

85. Neelakantan N, Narayanan M, de Souza RJ, van Dam RM. Effect of fenugreek (Trigonella foenum-graecumL.) intake on glycemia: a meta-analysis of clinical trials. Nutr J [Internet] 2014 [cited 2025 Mar 12];13(1):7. Available from: https://doi.org/10.1186/1475-2891-13-7

86. Jana K, Bera TK, Ghosh D. Antidiabetic effects of Eugenia jambolana in the streptozotocin-induced diabetic male albino rat. Biomark Genomic Med [Internet] 2015 [cited 2025 Feb 19];7(3):116–24. Available from: https://linkinghub.elsevier.com/retrieve/pii/S22140247 15000398

87. Gomaa AA, Farghaly HA, Abdel-Wadood YA, Gomaa GA. Potential therapeutic effects of boswellic acids/Boswellia serrata extract in the prevention and therapy of type 2 diabetes and Alzheimer's disease. Naunyn Schmiedebergs Arch Pharmacol [Internet]

2021 [cited 2025 Feb 19];394(11):2167–85. Available from: https://doi.org/10.1007/s00210-021-02154-7

88. Obadi M, Sun J, Xu B. Highland barley: Chemical composition, bioactive compounds, health effects, and applications. Food Res Int Ott Ont 2021;140:110065.

89. Deng N, Zheng B, Li T, Liu RH. Assessment of the Phenolic Profiles, Hypoglycemic Activity, and Molecular Mechanism of Different Highland Barley (Hordeum vulgare L.) Varieties. Int J Mol Sci [Internet] 2020 [cited 2025 Mar 13];21(4):1175. Available from: https://www.mdpi.com/1422-0067/21/4/1175

90. Effect of nutmeg on glycemic status in rat and mice: a systematic review [Internet]. CoLab [cited 2025 Mar 13];Available from: https://colab.ws/articles/10.1590%2Ffst.130122

91. Nasreen W, Sarker S, Sufian MA, Opo FADM, Shahriar M, Akhter R, et al. A possible alternative therapy for type 2 diabetes using Myristica fragrans Houtt in combination with glimepiride: in vivo evaluation and in silico support. Z Für Naturforschung C [Internet] 2020 [cited 2025 Mar 13];75(3–4):103–12. Available from: https://www.degruyter.com/document/doi/10.1515/znc-2019-0134/html

92. Faisal S, Tariq MH, Ullah R, Zafar S, Rizwan M, bibi N, et al. Exploring the antibacterial, antidiabetic, and anticancer potential of Mentha arvensis extract through in-silico and in-vitro analysis. BMC Complement Med Ther [Internet] 2023 [cited 2025 Feb 20];23(1):267. Available from: https://doi.org/10.1186/s12906-023-04072-y

93. Velmurugan C, Bhargava A. Anti-Diabetic activity of Gossypium Herbaceum by Alloxan Induced Model in Rats. 2(4).

94. Kulkarni CR, Joglekar MM, Patil SB, Arvindekar AU. Antihyperglycemic and antihyperlipidemic effect of Santalum album in streptozotocin induced diabetic rats. Pharm Biol [Internet] 2012 [cited 2025 Feb 23];50(3):360–5. Available from: https://doi.org/10.3109/13880209.2011.604677

95. Mohammadi S, Montasser Kouhsari S, Monavar Feshani A. Antidiabetic properties of the ethanolic extract of Rhus coriaria fruits in rats. DARU J Fac Pharm Tehran Univ Med Sci [Internet] 2010 [cited 2025 Feb 26];18(4):270–5. Available from: https://www.ncbi.nlm.nih.gov/pmc/articles/PMC3304353/

96. Chadchan KS, Jargar JG, Das SN. Anti-diabetic effects of aqueous prickly lettuce (Lactuca scariola Linn.) leaves extract in alloxan-induced male diabetic rats treated with nickel (II). J Basic Clin Physiol Pharmacol [Internet] 2016 [cited 2025 Feb 19];27(1):49–56. Available from: https://www.degruyter.com/document/doi/10.1515/jbcpp-2015-0038/html

97. Kabeeruddin M. Makhzanul Mufradat. New Delhi: Idara Kitabus Shifa; 2007.

98. Sinoriya P, Kaushik R, Sinoria A, Gaur PK. Comprehensive Review on Withania coagulans Dunal: Unveiling Pharmacognosy, Phytochemistry and Pharmacological Potentials. Pharmacogn Rev [Internet] 2024 [cited 2025 Feb 26];18(35):47–59. Available from: https://phcogrev.com/article/2024/18/35/105530phrev2024185

99. An Indian plant for diabetes control. Nat India [Internet] 2019 [cited 2025 Feb 26];Available from: https://www.nature.com/articles/nindia.2019.112

100. Sekar V, Chakraborty S, Mani S, Sali VK, Vasanthi HR. Mangiferin from Mangifera indica fruits reduces post-prandial glucose level by inhibiting α-glucosidase and α-amylase activity. South Afr J Bot [Internet] 2019 [cited 2025 Mar 12];120:129–34. Available from: https://www.sciencedirect.com/science/article/pii/S02 54629917315508

101. Ansari P, Flatt PR, Harriott P, Hannan JMA, Abdel-Wahab YH. Identification of multiple pancreatic and extra-pancreatic pathways underlying the glucose-lowering actions of Acacia arabica Bark in type-2 diabetes and isolation of active phytoconstituents. Plants [Internet] 2021 [cited 2025 Mar 12];10(6):1190. Available from: https://www.mdpi.com/2223-7747/10/6/1190

102. Vadivelan R, Krishnan RG, Kannan R. Antidiabetic potential of Asparagus racemosus Willd leaf extracts through inhibition of α-amylase and α-glucosidase. J Tradit Complement Med [Internet] 2019 [cited 2025 Mar 12];9(1):1–4. Available from: https://www.sciencedirect.com/science/article/pii/S22 25411017301268

103. Najib A. Acorus calamus L On Type 2 Diabetes Mellitus Medication. Univers J Pharm Res [Internet] 2020 [cited 2025 Mar 12];Available from: https://ujpronline.com/index.php/journal/article/view/3 91

104. Muñiz-Ramirez A, Perez RM, Garcia E, Garcia FE. Antidiabetic Activity of Aloe vera Leaves. Evid Based Complement Alternat Med [Internet] 2020 [cited 2025 Mar 12];2020(1):6371201. Available from: https://onlinelibrary.wiley.com/doi/10.1155/2020/6371 201

105. Putra WE, Hidayatullah A, Widiastuti D, Heikal MF, Salma WO. VIRTUAL SCREENING OF NATURAL ALPHA-GLUCOSIDASE INHIBITOR FROM ALPINIA GALANGA BIOACTIVE COMPOUNDS AS ANTI-DIABETIC CANDIDATE: ANTI-DIABETIC ACTIVITY OF ALPINIA GALANGA. J Microbiol Biotechnol Food Sci [Internet] 2023 [cited 2025 Mar 12];13(1):e4353–e4353. Available from: https://office2.jmbfs.org/index.php/JMBFS/article/view/4353

106. Gu S, Sun H, Zhang X, Huang F, Pan L, Zhu Z. Structural characterization and inhibitions on α-glucosidase and α-amylase of alkali-extracted water-soluble polysaccharide from Annona squamosa residue. Int J Biol Macromol [Internet] 2021 [cited 2025 Mar 12];166:730–40. Available from: https://www.sciencedirect.com/science/article/pii/S01 41813020348832

107. Amudhan M, Begum V. Alpha-glucosidase inhibitory and hypoglycemic activities of Areca catechu extract. Pharmacogn Mag [Internet] 2008 [cited 2025 Mar 12];4(15):223. Available from: https://www.researchgate.net/profile/Ajay-Padmawar/post/Is_there_aqueous_Areca_catechu_B etel_nuts_toxic_and_harmful_for_certain_cells/attach ment/59d6380279197b807799545b/AS%3A3956481 56356610%401471341279369/download/Alpha-glucosidase+inhibitory+and+hypoglycemic+activities+ of.pdf

108. Thant AA, Win YY, Khine MM, Than NN. IDENTIFICATION OF APIGENIN AND LUTEOLIN ISOLATED FROM THE AERIAL PARTS OF BACOPA MONNIERI (L.) WETTST IN VITRO EVALUATION OF α-AMYLASE AND α-GLUCOSIDASE INHIBITION ACTIVITY. [cited 2025 Mar 12];Available from:

http://maas.edu.mm/Research/Admin/pdf/17.%20Daw
%20Aye%20Aye%20Thant%20(169-180).pdf

109. El-Sayed ST, Jwanny EW, Rashad MM, Mahmoud AE, Abdallah NM. Glycosidases in plant tissues of some brassicaceae screening of different cruciferous plants for glycosidases production. Appl Biochem Biotechnol [Internet] 1995 [cited 2025 Mar 12];55(3):219–30. Available from: http://link.springer.com/10.1007/BF02786861

110. Harish M, Ahmed F, Urooj A. In vitro hypoglycemic effects of Butea monosperma Lam. leaves and bark. J Food Sci Technol [Internet] 2014 [cited 2025 Mar 12];51(2):308–14. Available from: http://link.springer.com/10.1007/s13197-011-0496-8

111. Naik S, Deora N, Pal SK, Ahmed MZ, Alqahtani AS, Shukla PK, et al. Purification, biochemical characterization, and DPP-IV and α-amylase inhibitory activity of Berberine from Cardiospermum halicacabum. J Mol Recognit JMR 2022;35(11):e2983.

112. Elshibani F, Alamami A, Alshalmani S, El Naili EA, Gehawe HA, Sharkasi MA, et al. Estimation of phenolic content, flavonoid content, antioxidant properties and alpha-amylase inhibitory activities of Capparis spinosa L. J Pharmacognocy Photochem [Internet] 2020 [cited 2025 Mar 12];9:24–8. Available from: https://www.academia.edu/download/89314734/9-3-451-668.pdf

113. Wajidi M, Vaid FH, Rizwani GH, Faiyaz A, Shareef H, Akram A, et al. Anti-Oxidant and digestive enzymes inhibitory based anti diabetic activity of crude and fractions of Carum carvi L. extracts. Pak J Pharm Sci [Internet] 2019 [cited 2025 Mar 12];32(6). Available from:

https://www.academia.edu/download/108041498/Paper-21.pdf

114. Kumar Chaudhary S, Kharlyngdoh E, Shukla JK, Bhardwaj PK, Thorat SS, Bhowmick S, et al. Antidiabetic and Antioxidant Activities of Indian Bay Leaf (Cinnamomum tamala (Buch.-Ham.) T. Nees & Eberm.) Essential Oils Collected from Meghalaya. Chem Biodivers [Internet] 2024 [cited 2025 Mar 12];21(11):e202400879. Available from: https://onlinelibrary.wiley.com/doi/10.1002/cbdv.2024 00879

115. Sriramavaratharajan V, Murugan R. Cumin scented leaf essential oil of Cinnamomum chemungianum : compositions and their in vitro antioxidant, α-amylase, α-glucosidase and lipase inhibitory activities. Nat Prod Res [Internet] 2018 [cited 2025 Mar 12];32(17):2081– 4. Available from: https://www.tandfonline.com/doi/full/10.1080/1478641 9.2017.1360884

116. Loizzo MR, Marrelli M, Pugliese A, Conforti F, Nadjafi F, Menichini F, et al. Crocus cancellatus subsp. damascenus stigmas: chemical profile, and inhibition of α -amylase, α -glucosidase and lipase, key enzymes related to type 2 diabetes and obesity. J Enzyme Inhib Med Chem [Internet] 2016 [cited 2025 Mar 12];31(2):212–8. Available from: https://www.tandfonline.com/doi/full/10.3109/1475636 6.2015.1016510

117. Fathima HM, Lakshmi Thangavelu LT, Anitha Roy AR. Anti-diabetic activity of Cassia fistula (alpha amylase-inhibitory effect). 2018 [cited 2025 Mar 12];Available from: https://www.cabidigitallibrary.org/doi/full/10.5555/201 93284266

118. Dalar A, Konczak I. Cichorium intybus from Eastern Anatolia: Phenolic composition, antioxidant and enzyme inhibitory activities. Ind Crops Prod [Internet] 2014 [cited 2025 Mar 12];60:79–85. Available from: https://www.sciencedirect.com/science/article/pii/S09 26669014003227

119. Wasana K, Attanayake A, Weerarathna K. Natural drug leads as novel DPP-IV inhibitors targeting the management of type 2 diabetes mellitus. J Complement Med Res [Internet] 2020 [cited 2025 Mar 12];11(1):43. Available from: https://ejmanager.com/fulltextpdf.php?mno=115987

120. Lekshmi PC, Arimboor R, Nisha VM, Menon AN, Raghu KG. In vitro antidiabetic and inhibitory potential of turmeric (Curcuma longa L) rhizome against cellular and LDL oxidation and angiotensin converting enzyme. J Food Sci Technol [Internet] 2014 [cited 2025 Mar 12];51(12):3910–7. Available from: http://link.springer.com/10.1007/s13197-013-0953-7

121. Sobhi W, Stevigny C, Duez P, Calderon BB, Atmani D, Benboubetra M. Effect of lipid extracts of Nigella sativa L. seeds on the liver ATP reduction and alpha-glucosidase inhibition. Pak J Pharm Sci [Internet] 2016 [cited 2025 Mar 12];29(1). Available from: https://www.researchgate.net/profile/Widad-Sobhi/publication/292163412_PEffect_of_lipid_extrac ts_of_Nigella_sativa_L_seeds_on_the_liver_ATP_red uction_and_alpha-glucosidase_inhibition/links/5a0ef1480f7e9bdf9111be d2/PEffect-of-lipid-extracts-of-Nigella-sativa-L-seeds-on-the-liver-ATP-reduction-and-alpha-glucosidase-inhibition.pdf

122. Boonpisuttinant K, Winitchai S, Akkarakultron P, Udompong S. In vitro alpha-glucosidase and alpha-amylase enzyme-inhibited activities by water-lily

(Nymphaea genus) extracts. Malays Appl Biol [Internet] 2019 [cited 2025 Mar 12];48(4):121–7. Available from: https://jms.mabjournal.com/index.php/mab/article/view/1886

123. Chen WC, Wang SW, Li CW, Lin HR, Yang CS, Chu YC, et al. Comparison of various solvent extracts and major bioactive components from Portulaca oleracea for antioxidant, anti-tyrosinase, and anti-α-glucosidase activities. Antioxidants [Internet] 2022 [cited 2025 Mar 12];11(2):398. Available from: https://www.mdpi.com/2076-3921/11/2/398

124. Gad-Elkareem MA, Abdelgadir EH, Badawy OM, Kadri A. Potential antidiabetic effect of ethanolic and aqueous-ethanolic extracts of Ricinus communis leaves on streptozotocin-induced diabetes in rats. PeerJ [Internet] 2019 [cited 2025 Mar 12];7:e6441. Available from: https://peerj.com/articles/6441/

125. Umamageswari MS, Karthikeyan TM, Maniyar YA. Antidiabetic activity of aqueous extract of Solanum nigrum linn berries in alloxan induced diabetic wistar albino rats. J Clin Diagn Res Jcdr [Internet] 2017 [cited 2025 Mar 12];11(7):FC16. Available from: https://pmc.ncbi.nlm.nih.gov/articles/PMC5583816/

126. Smina CS, Lalitha P, Nagabhushana H, Sharma SC. Terminalia bellirica dried fruit and seed extract offers alpha-amylase inhibitory potential in tackling diabetes. Appl Nanosci [Internet] 2020 [cited 2025 Mar 12];10(11):4325–39. Available from: https://link.springer.com/10.1007/s13204-020-01549-x

127. Das A, Naveen J, Sreerama YN, Gnanesh Kumar BS, Baskaran V. Low-glycemic foods with wheat, barley and herbs (Terminalia chebula, Terminalia bellerica

and Emblica officinalis) inhibit α-amylase, α-glucosidase and DPP-IV activity in high fat and low dose streptozotocin-induced diabetic rat. J Food Sci Technol [Internet] 2022 [cited 2025 Mar 12];59(6):2177–88. Available from: https://link.springer.com/10.1007/s13197-021-05231-0

128. Geethalakshmi R, Sarada DVL, Ramasamy K. Trianthema decandra L: a review on its phytochemical and pharmacological profile. Int J Eng Sci Technol [Internet] 2010 [cited 2025 Mar 12];2:976–9. Available from: https://www.researchgate.net/profile/Geethalakshmi-Rajarathinam/publication/50273879_Trianthema_decandra_L_A_review_on_its_phytochemical_and_pharmacological_profile/links/0c96053c36c861a8e7000000/Trianthema-decandra-L-A-review-on-its-phytochemical-and-pharmacological-profile.pdf

129. Khan MA, Khan H, Ali T. Withanolides isolated from Withania somnifera with α-glucosidase inhibition. Med Chem Res [Internet] 2014 [cited 2025 Mar 12];23(5):2386–90. http://link.springer.com/10.1007/s00044-013-0838-3